A Monetarist Model of
Inflationary Expectations

A Monetarist Model of Inflationary Expectations

John Rutledge
Tulane University

Lexington Books
D.C. Heath and Company
Lexington, Massachusetts
Toronto   London

Library of Congress Cataloging in Publication Data

Rutledge, John.
A monetarist model of inflationary expectations.

Includes bibliographical references.
1. Inflation (Finance)—Mathematical models. I. Title.
HG229.R87   332.4'1   73-22377
ISBN 0-669-92502-0

International Standard Book Number: 0-669-92502-0

Library of Congress Catalog Card Number: 73-22377

For Lou and Jessie

Contents

List of Figures   ix

List of Tables   xi

Preface   xiii

Acknowledgments   xv

Chapter 1   Introduction   1

Chapter 2   Review of Previous Work on Expectations   7

2.1 The Development of Rational Forecasting   7
2.2 Extrapolative Models of Inflation
    Forecasts   16

Chapter 3   Optimal Use of Information   29

3.1 Optimal Use of Information   30
3.2 Estimating Inflationary Expectations   34
3.3 Implicit Forward Interest Rates   37
3.4 Test Results   40
3.5 Evidence Concerning a Corollary
    Hypothesis   43
3.6 Further Extensions and Conclusions   44

Chapter 4   Rational Expectations of Inflation   47

4.1 Rational Expectations and
    Autoregressive Models   48
4.2 A Simple Model of Inflation   52
4.3 Rational Forecasts   55
4.4 The Crude Quantity Theory and
    Rational Expectations   61

4.5 Models with Autoregressive Real Rate   65
4.6 Conclusions   70

Chapter 5   **Announcement Effects and Rational Expectations**   73

5.1 Twisting the Term Structure   78
5.2 Operation Twist   79
5.3 "Twisting" and Rational Expectations   83
5.4 Achieving a "Target" Yield Curve   87
5.5 Conclusions   91

Chapter 6   **Conclusions**   93

Appendix   101

Notes   107

Index   117

About the Author   121

List of Figures

3-1   Optimal Combinations of Information Inputs   31

3-2   Marginal Costs and Returns to Information   33

5-1   The Term Structure of π^*_{t+k} 78

5-2   A Hypothetical Yield Curve   79

5-3   A Yield Curve and the Corresponding
        Marginal Yield Curve   84

5-4   A Real Marginal Yield Curve   85

5-5   A Set of Real and Nominal Marginal
        Yield Curves   86

List of Tables

3-1   Parameter Estimates of Equation (3.28)   41

3-2   Parameter Estimates of Equation (3.29)   42

4-1   Parameter Estimates of Equation (4.29)   57

4-2   Parameter Estimates of Equation (4.33)   58

4-3   Parameter Estimates of Equation (4.35)   60

4-4   Parameter Estimates of Equation (4.52)   63

4-5   Parameter Estimates of Equation (4.51)   64

4-6   Parameter Estimates of Equation (4.49)   65

4-7   Statistics from Estimates of Models Adopting
           the Autoregressive Real Rate Assumption
           (4.55)   68

Preface

The positive rates of inflation in most of the major countries in the past decade have resulted in a shift of emphasis away from the problems of unemployment and stagnation, and toward the problems that arise in an inflationary economy. Economists have been especially interested in the effects on certain economic variables if investors come to *expect* inflation. The relation between inflationary expectations and market interest rates has long been realized, but price expectations variables have begun to appear in more and more research, in both theoretical and empirical models.

In order to test the theories incorporating price expectations, one must be able to measure them, yet they are *per se* unobservable magnitudes. The solution has been, almost invariably, to posit a relationship between expectations of inflation and nominal rates of interest, then explain interest rates with variables assumed to be important in the formation of expectations to get a proxy for the expected rate of inflation. The models reveal a touch of schizophrenia on the part of their builders. Economists want to acknowledge that expectations will be formed, because it is in the interest of rational profit-maximizing investors to do so. In contrast, the models typically specify forecasting mechanisms that are totally ad hoc, generally assuming that investors form forecasts autoregressively. Since there are many additional sources of information about the future rate of inflation (economists do not rely on simple autoregressive models of inflation), it is possible that investors utilize other sources in addition to past rates of inflation. The result, of course, depends on the costs and rewards of doing so. To my knowledge, no careful analysis of investor forecasting, focusing on profit-maximizing behavior in the choice of forecasting mechanism, exists in the literature today. Since incorrect specification of forecasting mechanisms will introduce specification errors into all econometric models using them, the lack of consistent treatment of forecasting by the economics literature is a serious deficiency.

The book attempts first to examine profit-maximizing behavior in the production of forecasts and to reveal important properties of the forecasting mechanism. Then I examine revealed forecasts in order to identify the particular sources of information exploited by investors. Next we consider a more restrictive assumption, "Rational Expectations," which says that the world can be treated as if costs of collecting information were essentially zero. Finally we examine implications for certain questions in capital theory which have special relevance to policy decisions. The evidence presented in this book indicates that the deficiency in the treatment of expectations by economists is a serious one and it suggests the way to much additional research in this area.

Acknowledgments

This study has benefited from criticism of many friends and instructors over the past two years. My greatest debt is to Bennett T. McCallum, who taught me that in testing hypotheses, models which are supposed to represent the behavior of rational individuals should, at the very least, be consistent with utility-maximizing behavior. Professor McCallum contributed many helpful comments at every stage of the work. Professor Richard T. Selden was most helpful at several extremely troublesome stages. Chapter 3 has benefited from criticisms of an earlier draft by Milton Friedman, Robert Barro, and Robert Gordon, as well as other members of the Workshop in Money and Banking at the University of Chicago, where I spent a term in residence. The work presented in Chapter 4 bears the unmistakable mark of a paper by Charles Nelson[a] and of discussions of that paper with Nelson during the Fall of 1972. Lengthy discussions of this Chapter with Robert J. Barro also resulted in a much better product. Comments on Chapter 5 by David Meiselman were helpful.

Special thanks are given to my wife, Lou. It is undoubtedly true that this book would never have been completed without her constant encouragement and buoyant optimism.

Financial support for this study is gratefully acknowledged. Early research was supported by a grant from the Earhart Foundation. The research was completed and the dissertation written while the author was a Harold Stonier Fellow of the American Bankers Association.

Finally, I would like to acknowledge my debt to my typist, Mrs. Vicki Leonhard. Her patience while struggling with a difficult and often illegible manuscript resulted in a finished product ahead of schedule.

Though many of the individuals mentioned above are responsible for suggestions which substantially improved the analysis and exposition of this study, I did not accept all of their suggestions. Responsibility for remaining errors and omissions remains entirely with the author.

---

[a]Charles Nelson, "The Structure of Rational Expectations: Implications for the Predictive Efficiency of Economic Models and the Empirical Specification of Expectations Mechanisms," (Mimeographed, University of Chicago, 1972).

1 Introduction

En fait, le problème de l'intérêt constitue certainement le problème le plus ardu de la science économique et l'utilité de son étude est absolument fondamentale.[1]

Maurice Allais

The emergence of inflation in most of the major countries in the West since the end of World War II, and the policy problems which accompany inflation, have given rise to renewed interest in the relationship between the rate of inflation and the market rate of interest. This relation is explained largely by the fact that investors form forecasts of future rates of inflation which enter as explanatory variables into their demand and supply schedules for real capital. The importance of distinguishing between real and nominal rates of interest was understood long before this time, of course. In *Value and Capital*, for instance, Hicks wrote:

... the real economist, working with his auxiliary standard, only determining values in terms of that and paying no attention to the value of money, cannot get to grips with the rate of interest. Unless he looks very carefully where he is going, he will find himself not determining the true rate of interest, which (as we have seen) is a money rate, but the only rate of interest which is contained in his limited system—a rate indicating the value of future deliveries of the auxiliary commodity in terms of current deliveries of the same auxiliary standard.

Now there is no reason why this natural rate (as we may call it, following Wicksell) should be the same as the true 'money' rate of interest. As we have seen, they will be identical only if futures prices of the auxiliary commodity are the same as spot prices. This condition will be fulfilled if the value of money (or the money value of the auxiliary standard commodity) is not expected to change at all, and if this expectation is absolutely certain, so that risk is absent.[2]

Since that time, though, macromodels designed to formalize the Keynesian system have largely neglected this consideration, perhaps due to the Keynesian conception of the world as characterized by unemployment and sticky prices. Harry Johnson remarks:

The Keynesian system often assumes a constant price level; this has theoretical advantages; for it ascribes to money the unique property of safety so that it can be used as the anchor of the system. But if that assumption is not justified, then ignoring price expectations will result in faulty analysis and prediction.[3]

1

Many economists, especially those referred to as "Monetarists," have viewed the experience of the past few decades as evidence that this assumption is, indeed, not justified. It has been recognized that precise measurement and understanding of inflation expectations deserve much analysis and thought. Accordingly, the list of research papers published in this area has risen to meet the increased demand. Variables representing the expected rate of inflation have been introduced into existing theories to adapt them to a world of changing prices. For example, this variable is now widely recognized as being important in the demand for money, having an important influence on nominal rates of interest, and influencing the alleged tradeoff between the rate of unemployment and the rate of inflation. Studies in this area have largely been designed to test these theories against alternatives which do not depend on the existence of inflationary expectations, and to test alternative models of the mechanism by which investors form their forecasts of the rate of inflation. Existing studies, however, exhibit a remarkable degree of conformity in one respect. The hypotheses typically examined concerning forecasting mechanisms all belong to the "weak-form," or autoregressive class. Investors are assumed to base their forecasts only on information contained in the past history of the rate of inflation. Equivalently, people in the market are viewed as time series analysts, who exploit the serial correlation properties of the realized inflation series in producing forecasts. The existence and availability of other types of information which might be collected and processed into forecasts by investors is occasionally recognized, but seldom explicitly introduced into either theoretical or empirical models intended to reproduce investor behavior.

It is widely recognized that, if relevant explanatory variables are omitted from econometric models, the errors in specification generally result in biased and inconsistent estimates of all parameters in the model.[a] Hence, if investors' expectations of inflation are actually formed in a more sophisticated manner than usually granted in empirical studies, tests of hypotheses about the effects of expectations on various economic magnitudes will yield misleading results. For example, several tests have been performed which claimed to analyze the accelerationist theory of inflation. In that theory, rates of change in wages or prices are hypothesized to depend on (1) the rate of unemployment or capacity utilization and (2) the expected rate of inflation over the relevant future period. A test of this theory usually rests on the coefficient of the expectations variable. Thus, for example, Turnovsky and Wachter write:

... The absence of money illusion implies that these expectational variables should enter the wage equation with a coefficient equal to unity.[4]

---

[a]This result holds if the omitted variable(s) is (are) correlated with other exogenous variables in the model. When these variables are orthogonal to the omitted variable(s), however, resulting estimates are inefficient, but consistent and unbiased.

Obviously, if the variables used to represent expectations are unsatisfactory, the results of such tests will be suspect.

Many economists argue that it is important to test these theories properly:

Empirical verification of price-expectation affects warrants more attention, not only to substantiate the theory, but also as a guide in formulating and evaluating national economic policy.[5]

It follows that we should examine our expectations models carefully, to see that specification errors are not present.

The problem addressed in this study is the validity of models representing expected rates of inflation as a weighted sum of past realized rates. Since many other types of information are available to investors at finite collection cost, and since we know that there exist more reliable theories of future inflation than extrapolative theories, it is possible that investors incorporate these same sources of information into their forecasts. The use of such information depends essentially on the costs of collection relative to the "marginal return" in the form of higher profits due to increased forecast accuracy. Assuming that certain classes of information are not incorporated into forecasts, is equivalent to an assumption that these classes of information are so expensive that it does not pay the investor to exploit them. We shall show in Chapter 3, in the context of a two-period model of intertemporal wealth allocation that explicitly introduces costs of and returns to searching for information, that the properties of the first-order conditions for efficiency make it extremely likely that all information that has predictive value will be exploited. This result is due to inherent economies of scale in combining individual portfolios to gather information.

Since we will argue that it is likely that investors will process multiple sources of information in forming profit-maximizing forecasts, it will be of some interest to look for an explanation for the almost universal use of autoregressive hypotheses of forecast formation. Chapter 2 deals precisely with this point, tracing the development of expectations models through its major stages. We will argue that the idea of investors choosing to process additional information is not new, but was held by both Alfred Marshall and John Maynard Keynes, and was central to their theories of the rate of interest and the business cycle. Although Fisher was one of the first to recognize the importance of expectations of inflation, we will show that Fisher held different views about the behavior of investors. In particular, we will show that he considered the adjustment of the market rate of interest to a change in inflation to be an indirect one, and not due to conscious forecasts. When he analyzed the relation between inflation and the money rate of interest, he emphasized that he was not solely measuring expectational effects, but the total impact of inflation on the rate of interest, which largely worked through alterations in prices and profit levels and the volume of trade. In other words, he meant to estimate a relation similar to Wicksell's cumulative process. Most modern writers interpret the equations estimated by Fisher in the more restrictive sense of forecasts of inflation, and specify their models of the forecasting mechanism after the equations estimated by Fisher for a related, but different purpose.

In 1961, a notable paper by John F. Muth[6] appeared in *Econometrica*. This paper broke cleanly with the well-established extrapolative tradition by emphasizing that investors have incentives to gather many types of information, and that, given certain cost structures, they will choose to collect information on the process generating the series to be forecast. Muth likened the activities of investors to those of professional economists; both face given costs of collecting and processing information, and both will be rewarded if their forecasts prove quite accurate. It is possible, then, that investors forecast *as if* they were aware of the structure of the market in question. This leads to the obvious conclusion that investors will find it valuable to collect information on values of exogenous variables in such structures and incorporate these values into their forecasts in a manner similar to the econometrician's reduced-form equations.

It might be expected that the appearance of Muth's paper would have set off a wave of studies similar to this one, trying to test hypotheses of forecast formation and gathering evidence on the kinds of information that investors find worthwhile to incorporate into their predictions of the rate of inflation. Unfortunately, this was not the case. In the example chosen by Muth to illustrate the concept of "rational expectations," the optimal predictor was reduced to extrapolative form. This result gave great confidence to those employing weak-form hypotheses of forecast formation because it provided a theory apparently showing that this is the way in which rational individuals would behave. This view, of course, is largely erroneous, as will be demonstrated in Chapter 4. In a model with more than one exogenous input, rational expectations cannot be expressed in extrapolative form. This misinterpretation of Muth's model reinforced the growing number of extrapolative models in the literature. It is in the aim of Chapter 2 to correct this view.

In Chapter 3 we will formalize the behavior of a profit-maximizing investor to include costly information collection and processing. We point out the conditions under which an investor will collect information in a two-period certainty model in which the investor faces given incomes in periods 1 and 2, given initial assets, a given market rate of interest, and cost and return functions for information processing activities. He then must choose his level of consumption in period 1 and the amount of information which he chooses to buy in order to increase the rate of return on his investment. The properties of the solution of the investor's problem allow for economies of scale, which suggest that it may be profitable to combine with other investors in information search activities. This also leads us to predict that, if such cooperation actually takes place, a much larger fraction of total available information will be incorporated into forecasts and hence will be reflected in market supply and demand schedules and market prices.

In a later section of Chapter 3, we will develop a simple model of forecast formation which assumes that investors gather information about past behavior of the money supply, as well as the past history of inflation, in making their predictions. This model is tested against an alternative model in which expectations are formed extrapolatively, with no knowledge of money stock changes in previous periods. The test is accomplished by utilizing the Fisher relation between nominal rates of interest and the expected rate of inflation. A forward rate of interest, implicit in the term structure of nominal interest rates, is used as a measure of the "expected" rate of interest in a future period under the assumption of the unbiased expectations theory of the term structure. The latter is employed for at least two reasons: (1) it lessens the estimation problem due to the short-term relation between money and interest known as the liquidity effect, and (2) it will facilitate much of the work to be carried out in Chapters 4 and 5 on related matters. Tests are also carried out in this chapter using various "spot" or market rates of interest, with similar results. In every case the hypothesis of extrapolative expectations is rejected in favor of the more general hypothesis that investors also process information about money growth, which we shall call "consistent expectations."

Chapter 4 is aimed specifically at testing alternative methods of rational expectations against models in which forecasts are not formed rationally. Several structural models of the process generating inflation are specified and their corresponding reduced-form equations derived. It is then hypothesized that market participants form expectations *as if* they were aware of the structure. In every case, using a variety of rates of interest (both spot and forward) and alternative assumptions about the real rate of interest, market expectations are shown to be indistinguishable from rational expectations derived from a model with zero information costs. The tests performed in this chapter are much more restrictive than those in Chapter 3 and accordingly provide greater support for rational forecasting. We also have occasion to examine in some detail recent work on rational expectations, comparing our results with those of other writers.

Chapter 5 is designed to develop, in greater depth, corollaries of the hypotheses tested in the earlier chapters. The model of rational expectations implies that, under certain assumptions about the stochastic behavior of the exogenous processes entering the structural model, it may pay investors to gather information about their future behavior as well. This information will yield probabilistic statements about the future path of, say, the rate of growth of the money supply. One major source of information about future monetary actions is current announcements of the stabilization authorities. In this chapter, the precise relationship between announcements of the Federal Reserve and the term structure of predictions of inflation is examined. This implies a corresponding relationship between announcements and the "marginal" term-to-maturity structure of interest rates. A model of inflation is presented in which the assumptions of the stochastic behavior of the money growth series are relaxed to allow for announcement effects.

Having established a theoretical link between central bank behavior and the term structure of nominal interest rates, based entirely upon the expectations theory of the term structure, we discuss an earlier attempt of the Federal Reserve to alter the shape and position of the yield curve, namely "Operation Twist." This effort was based on an entirely different view of investor behavior, in which markets were considered segmented by institutional constraints on investor behavior. It is shown that by properly choosing the announcements made, if they are credible, "twisting" is entirely consistent with the spirit of the expectations hypothesis, and, indeed, is implied once we introduce rational forecasting.

Chapter 6 sums up the main conclusions of the analysis with respect to tests of alternative expectations hypotheses, lags in expectation formation, and behavior of the Federal Reserve vis-à-vis announcements. Suggestions for further analysis are presented. The most promising lines of research seem to involve development of (1) more detailed structural models of inflation, and (2) a more satisfactory treatment of the real rate of interest. A model specifying the structure of the process generating the real rate of return, hence leading to a rational forecast of the real rate of return, would go a long way toward supplying this deficiency. Finally, applications of the analysis of this study to various policy matters are considered, especially with respect to the case for a monetary rule and efficacy of incomes policies in controlling inflation.

To sum up, then, the theme of this book is that recent research into the causes and effects of expectations of inflation has been heading in the wrong direction. Rather than attempt to develop more sophisticated theories of the effects of expectations of inflation on other variables, I maintain that our most urgent need is to understand the sources of information incorporated into forecasts by market traders. This is best accomplished by detailed examination of the costs and incentives of forecast production within the context of a model of profit-maximizing behavior on the part of the investor, similar to the one presented in Chapter 3. The goal of such research is more accurate measurement of market expectations of inflation, which will facilitate and strengthen tests of hypotheses in which expectations enter as explanatory variables. Unfortunately, work in this area has been proceding slowly, and many questions remain to be analyzed. This study looks at only a small subset of these questions.

It is hoped that this study contributes toward eliminating "theoretical ad-hockery" in models of expectations formation, and toward the reestablishment of rationality—the "sine qua non of economic theory"[7]—in economic treatments of forecasting.

2 Review of Previous Work on Expectations

The analysis presented in this study is a logical extension of a school of thought that has its roots in the writings of John Locke, and which was developed by such economists as Alfred Marshall, John Maynard Keynes and, more recently, John F. Muth, A.A. Walters, Charles Nelson, and Robert Mundell. For brevity I shall refer to this approach to the subject as "rational expectations." A sharply contrasting approach has grown out of the work of Irving Fisher. The bulk of recent empirical work on inflation expectations has been produced by this second school, whose members include Phillip Cagan, Milton Friedman, Thomas Sargent, William Gibson, William Yohe, Denis Karnosky, Martin Feldstein, and Otto Eckstein. The common element in the work of this latter group of writers is their assumption that individuals form forecasts of a variable only by examining the serial correlation properties of its past behavior. Much of the analysis presented in this book is an attempt to show that this assumption is not justified.

The purpose of this chapter is to review earlier work on price expectations so that the results of Chapters 3, 4, and 5 can be viewed in historical perspective. The literature on rational expectations is surveyed in Section 2.1, that on autoregressive expectations in Section 2.2.

2.1 The Development of Rational Forecasting

The basic tenet of consistent expectations and rational expectations is that individuals will find it to their advantage to gather information about the way the economy generates inflation, and on the most important variables in that process, in order to form more accurate forecasts of the future course of inflation. This view of forecast formation is not new but, rather, has enjoyed a long and rich history in the economics literature. The purpose of this brief survey is to show that a number of prominent writers have advanced explanations of inflation forecasts similar to those presented in this study, and that these explanations have largely been neglected in recent work in this area.

In the next chapter a model is presented which treats forecasting as a production activity. Forecasts are produced by combining various amounts of inputs (types of information and labor, etc.). The decision of how to forecast inflation optimally will be shown to depend upon the costs of collecting and processing the various types of information and on the production function relating the inputs to some measure of forecast accuracy. The particular form of this production function depends upon the investor's view of the world. The investor observes certain regularities in his environment, and incorporates them into the production function. Then, depending upon the costs of collecting and processing this information, and the increased gains from doing so, the information may be reflected in the investor's (revised) forecasts of inflation. Although recently this proposition has been the focus of revived interest, it was clearly asserted as early as 1689 by John Locke in his *An Essay Concerning Human Understanding*. One scholar wrote of this essay:

His *Essay Concerning Human Understanding* is concerned precisely with epistemology, or the theory of knowledge. . . . As a philosopher of understanding in the British empirical tradition begun by Bacon and continued by Hume and Mill, Locke reasoned that man learned only through his senses. Man was a *tabula rasa* with no innate ideas. As it was in his own interest to do whatever would permit him to avoid pain and increase his gains, he would learn about the world by experience.[1]

Locke included a discussion of the way in which ideas of relations are altered, i.e., the way in which the production function of forecasts is changed in a world of uncertainty.[a]

Modern economists, of course, largely agree with this interpretation of how individuals learn, and how they produce forecasts. Nevertheless, most recent work employing autoregressive forecasting models implicitly adopts ad hoc assumptions about the form of the forecast production function and costs of certain types of information. They typically assume that the only type of information that investors will choose to collect and process is past values of the time series being forecast. I maintain that the subset of available information which investors use is somewhat larger than these models imply, including

---

[a]Locke describes how individuals must at times act on scanty information: "He that will not eat till he has demonstration that it will nourish him, he that will not stir till he infallibly knows the business he goes about will succeed, will have little else to do but sit still and perish."[2] Individuals form impressions from their experiences: "Probability, then, being to supply the defect of our knowledge, and to guide us where that fails, is always conversant about propositions whereof we have no certainty, but only some inducement to receive them for true. The grounds for it are, in short, these two following: First the conformity of anything with our *knowledge, observation* and *experience*. Secondly, the testimony of others, vouching their *observation* and *experience*."[3] And of regularities which are obvious for long periods of time (which we will call on later to be the long-observed relation between money and prices) Locke states: "This we call an argument from the nature of things themselves. For what our own and other men's constant observation has always found to be after the same manner, that we with reason conclude to be the *effects of steady and regular causes, though they come not within the reach of our knowledge.* These probabilities rise so near to certainty, that they govern our thoughts as absolutely, and influence all our actions as fully, as the most evident demonstration; and in what concerns us we make little or no difference between them and certain knowledge. Our belief, thus grounded, rises to assurance."[4] It is not necessary, then, for investors to attend graduate school in order to understand some of the plainer workings of the market place.

information on relevant exogenous variables combining to determine the rate of inflation in our economic models.

Alfred Marshall played a prominent role in the early development of Rational Expectations. Marshall held that expectations of both profits and changes in the value of money were instrumental in the reaction of the market rate of interest to changes in the quantity of money:

... the influx of a little extra gold, going as it does into the hands of those who deal in credit, causes the supply to rise relative to the demand; the rate of discount falls below its equilibrium level, however low that was, and therefore stimulates speculation. ... whatever form their speculation may take, it is almost sure, directly or indirectly, to raise prices. This is the main issue. There is, however, a side issue which may be in some cases more important than the main issue. It is that, *when the gold comes to the country its arrival is known, and people expect that prices will rise a little.* Now if a person doubting whether to borrow for speculative purposes has reason to believe that prices will rise, he is willing to take a loan at 3 percent, which before he would not have taken at more than 2-1/2 percent. Consequently, *the influx of gold into the country, by making people believe that prices will rise,* increases the demand over currency, as means of buying goods; and thus profiting by a rise in price. It tends therefore to raise discount.[5]

Later in Book IV on "Fluctuations in Business" Marshall states:

... the influx of a good deal of bullion into the city is likely to lower the level of discount. When this has been done there is more capital in the hands of speculative investors, who come on the market for goods as buyers, and so raise prices. *Further the influx of bullion, will have caused people to expect a raise in prices,* and therefore to be more inclined to borrow for speculative investments ... causing a rise in the rate of discount.[6]

Marshall contended that investors and bankers would be aware of the relationship between changes in the quantity of money and the price level, not because they had studied this in the classroom but simply through intuition based on long experience in attempting to maximize wealth.

The importance of the direct link between central bank actions and expectations of inflation was emphasized in the writings of Marshall's intellectual descendant, J.M. Keynes. This is especially notable[b] in his *A Treatise on Money.* For example, in his discussion of the behavior of entrepreneurs, Keynes states:

Strictly, therefore, we should say that it is the anticipated profit or loss which is the mainspring of change, and that it is by causing anticipations of the appropriate kind that the banking system is able to influence the price level. Indeed it is well known that *one reason for the rapid efficacy of changes in bank rate in modifying the actions of entrepreneurs is the anticipations to which they*

[b]See, notably, Chapters 11, 13, 17, 18 in Vol. I.

give rise. Thus entrepreneurs will sometimes begin to act before the price changes which are the justification of their action have actually occurred.[7]

Later in the same chapter Keynes remarks:

All the same, accurate forecasting in these matters is so difficult and requires so much more information than is usually available, that the average behavior of entrepreneurs in fact is mainly governed by current experience supplemented by such broad generalizations as those relating to the *probable consequences of changes in the bank rate, the supply of credit and the state of the foreign exchanges.* Moreover, actions based on inaccurate anticipations will not long survive experiences of a contrary character, so that the facts will soon override anticipations except where they agree.[8]

In Chapter 13, "The 'Modus Operandi' of the Bank Rate," Keynes discusses the effects of monetary actions on the rate of investment in fixed capital:

... Now a change in the bank-rate ... may conceivably affect the prospective price of the real yield (from fixed capital), but only, as a rule, on goods the future yields of which will be spread over a comparatively short period of time *and if the change in bank-rate constitutes a new fact in itself—by throwing new light, for example, on the policy and intentions of the currency authority.*[9]

And again:

... as we have hinted above, a change in bank-rate may itself alter the natural rate of interest in the opposite direction to that in which the bank-rate has been changed, by altering expectations as to the future course of prices. For example, if bank-rate falls, this tends to raise the natural rate of interest, if it arouses expectations of a tendency toward rising prices, thus increasing the attractiveness of investment in terms of money.[10]

In a later discussion Keynes uses the term "monetary expectations" to refer to the above effect.

While remarking on the monetary causes of a disequilibrium in the purchasing power of money Keynes writes of the consequences of an "increase in the quantity of cash." Keynes notes that:

Certain entrepreneurs may now be willing to increase their output even if this means making higher offers than before to the factors of production because (as the ultimate result of the influx of new money) they foresee profits.[11]

These few passages from the *Treatise on Money* suffice to give the flavor of Keynes' view of speculators and investors as forecasters. Keynes viewed market participants as rational individuals, reacting to the incentives of profit maximization to gather and process information about the behavior of the monetary authorities to form their forecasts of the rate of inflation.

Since the late nineteen-thirties, the concept of rational expectations of inflation is noticeably absent from the literature until 1961 when John F. Muth published an article on "Rational Expectations and the Theory of Price Movements."[12] The main contribution of Muth's article is his recognition that investors have incentives to collect information about the structure that generates the variable being forecast. If, for example, the world is such that a change in the supply of money is always followed by a change in prices in the same direction with a lag, and if traders who make correct forecasts of inflation realize higher profits than those who do not, then it will pay investors—if information is sufficiently cheap—to learn of the empirical regularity between money and prices. They will incorporate this into their forecast production functions and will decide which types of information are worthwhile to collect, given the existing costs of collection and use. Muth recognized the formal similarity between the forecasts made by professional economists and those made by investors:

I should like to suggest that expectations, since they are informed predictions of future events, are essentially the same as the predictions of the relevant economic theory. At the risk of confusing this purely descriptive hypothesis with a pronouncement as to what firms ought to do, we call such expectations 'rational' . . . The hypothesis can be rephrased a little more precisely as follows: that expectations of firms (or, more generally, the subjective probability distributions of outcomes) tend to be distributed, for the same information set, about the prediction of the theory (or the 'objective' probability distributions of outcomes).[13]

Muth was quick to point out that this hypothesis did not presume that individual traders had been formally trained as economists:

It does not state that the scratchwork of entrepreneurs resembles the system of equations in any way; nor does it state that predictions of entrepreneurs are perfect or that their expectations are all the same.[14]

The argument is the same as the one used by Machlup in his famous controversy with Richard Lester on the realism of marginal analysis of the firm. Or as Friedman puts it, a champion billiard player can be treated *as if* he has a thorough grasp of differential equations. The fact that he never got through high school is wholly irrelevant.

The implications of the hypothesis of rational expectations, according to Muth, are:

... (1) Information is scarce, and the economic system generally does not waste it. (2) The way expectations are formed depends specifically on the structure of the relevant system describing the economy. (3) A public prediction in the sense of Grunberg and Modigliani will have no substantial effect on the operation of the economic system (unless it is based on inside information).[15]

An illustration of rational forecasting will be useful at this point. Let Y_t be an endogenous variable whose future value is to be forecast and let X and Z be vectors of past observations on the exogenous variables X_t and Z_t. Let the process generating Y_t be such that;

$$Y_t = f(X,Z). \tag{2.1}$$

A rational forecast of Y_t is formed by taking the expected value of (2.1) based on all available information on X and Z. In general the forecast will depend on past values of both X and Z; as we will see in Chapter 4, it cannot be reduced to an autoregressive forecast. Unfortunately, Muth chose to illustrate the hypothesis of rational expectations with a model having only one exogenous variable, e.g., $Y_t = g(X)$. In such a model the rational expectation, though still expressed as a function of past values of X_t, is reducible to an extrapolative forecast $Y_t = h(Y_{t-1}, \ldots, Y_{t-n})$. Had Muth chosen a more general model he would not have arrived at this result.[c] This gave great confidence to those who had been employing extrapolative specifications in their models of the formation of expectations, for it seemed to provide a theoretical justification for the previously *ad hoc* forecasting mechanisms. As Charles Nelson pointed out:

... the adjective 'rational' has degenerated in current usage to little more than a synonym for unbiased. The implicit assumption that rational expectations are autoregressive is reflected in the almost universal and unquestioned use of autoregressive expectations mechanisms in both econometric and purely theoretical models.[16]

Chapter 4 of this study attempts to reformulate and test a model of inflation expectations which is consistent with the spirit of Muth's original article.

A.A. Walters is one of the few economists who has attempted to develop and extend the work begun by Muth in 1961. In his "Consistent Expectations, Distributed Lags and the Quantity Theory,"[17] Walters briefly sketched how one might apply Muth's rational expectations hypothesis to the demand for money to account for expected price levels.[d] He first noted that "It is convenient to

[c]This result is illustrated in Section 4.1 of Chapter 4.

[d]Walters referred to the expectations of his model as "Consistent Expectations" to refer to the idea that expectations are consistent with the relevant economic theory. Interestingly enough, Walters mentions Muth's paper only in a footnote, where he attributes the concept of Rational Expectations to Richard Muth rather than to the author, John F. Muth.[18]

represent expected values as a weighted average of the past observed values of a variable,"[19] but he proceeded to complain about this approach:

If expected prices are determined by history, there is no separate role to be played by current economic events. Yet it is well known that such events do indeed affect current expectations. There is no waiting for history. Consider, for example, the consequences of an increase in the quantity of money within the simple quantity theory model. . . .

The question one might reasonably put is: Why do people continue to ignore the increase in the quantity of money when they formulate their expectations (of price change). Clearly if the quantity theory is perfect then to ignore the increase in the money supply is quite irrational—one would lose a lot of potential profit by closing one's eyes to the obvious. Those who used the quantity theory would triumph over those who did not. Even if the quantity theory were not perfect but were merely the theory that predicted better than any alternative theory, those who formulated their expectations using that theory would clearly make more profit than those who were unsophisticated extrapolators. *In principle one would expect profit-maximizing expectations to emerge from the structure; the best theory would win.*[20]

Walters recognized that in a world where information is not costless to collect and process, and where some types of information are very costly relative to others, the theory using the less costly information might be used by forecasters. But he saw no basis for assuming that information on monetary actions is especially costly relative to information on price behavior:

In the rest of this note I shall assume that the information costs are the same for all theories. Thus we are led to consider profit maximizing expectations in the context of a monetary model. The assumptions about the expectation process then are the same as those we normally make for micro-behavior. To give a short name to these profit maximizing expectations we shall call them consistent expectations.[21]

Walters then presents a simple model in which (1) the price level is determined by last period's money stock and the expected rate of price changes and (2) investors and money holders are aware of this process whereby the price level is determined. Walters reduced this model to an equation in which the current price level is determined by (1) last period's money stock and (2) the price level of last period. These expectations are consistent because:

evidence adduced from observing the realized values (of price level and money stock) will not, on the average, contradict the expectations formulated by this model.[22]

He then constructed a similar model in which expectations were assumed to be formed extrapolatively (by a geometric lag) and showed that the actual behavior of prices in this model is a function of the values of the money stock and the price level in both period $t - 1$ and $t - 2$. Thus Walters observed:

Clearly the actual course of prices is influenced by changes in the quantity of money and we cannot obtain changes in price series that reflects only past changes in prices. *Observations of events will discredit the extrapolative hypothesis.*[23]

Walter concludes with a comment on the effect of economic research on the system:

Consistent expectations pose an interesting methodological problem. If economic research does establish the efficacy of the quantity theory, then such research itself will generate a theory of expectations that will change the parameters of the system. Involvement is complete.[24]

Walters' main contribution in this article was his explicit recognition that if expectations held by investors are inconsistent with the data they observe in the market, they will alter the mechanism of expectations formation so that their predictions will agree with their observations. Clearly, rational expectations fit this condition of consistency. Walters' main contribution, I believe, is the application of the framework developed by Muth to the problem of the demand for money. Unfortunately, Walters did not proceed with the rigorous development of expectations models, nor did he perform empirical tests. The models developed and tested in Chapter 3 of this study are an attempt to extend Walters' analysis.

A more recent contributor to the literature on rational expectations is Charles R. Nelson. He hinted at the problem that concerns us in his award-winning, *The Term Structure of Interest Rates,*[25] and continued his investigation of the relationship between rational expectations and extrapolative models in an unpublished paper.[26] Nelson was interested in the implications of Muth's hypothesis of rational expectations for models of forecast formation. Muth's analysis suggested that market participants will find it to their advantage to learn about the structure of the process generating the variable being forecast, suggesting that models of forecasting wishing to reflect rational expectations should include elements of the structure of the model, with forecasts based upon exogenous variables in the structure. Nelson was puzzled by the almost universal use of autoregressive assumptions in models of forecast formation; he hypothesized that this is due to an improper generalization of Muth's results.

In the heuristic model of a market which Muth used as an illustration, the rational expectation of price turned out to be simply a weighted sum of past prices, that is, an autoregressive prediction. Since a purely statistical analysis of the price series would have revealed the same prediction scheme, it is not at all clear from Muth's example how, or even whether, knowlege of economic structure imparts information which is of value in forming expectations.[27]

Nelson shows that the model presented by Muth implies that p_t, the current market price, is equal to a discrete linear stochastic process in the *white noise*[e] disturbance process $\{u_t\}$ and can be expressed in pure autoregressive form as:

$$p_t = \sum_{i=1}^{\infty} \pi_i p_{t-i} + w_t \tag{2.2}$$

where the π_i are constants and $\{w_t\}$ is also a white noise process. It follows immediately that the rational expectation of price in period t, conditional upon information available in period $t - 1$, can be represented either by (1) a weighted sum of past values of the $\{u_t\}$ process or (2) a form which depends only on past prices:

$$p_t^* = \sum_{i=1}^{\infty} \pi_i p_{t-i}. \tag{2.3}$$

Nelson remarked that:

This result followed directly from the fact that p_t could be expressed as a weighted sum of the $\{u_t\}$ only. In the original model, then, (1) the rational expectation of price depends only on past prices, and (2) the structure of the market serves only to determine the parameters of (the) linear process generating p_t, and hence the optimal prediction weights π_i. A time series analyst, armed only with the past history of prices, would therefore be able to infer the π_i directly from $\{p_t\}$ and thereby *replicate the rational expectation of price without benefit of any knowledge of the market structure.*[28]

Clearly if this were the general case there would never be reason to gather information about the structure of the process which generates the variable forecast, or data on any of the exogenous processes entering the structure. Nelson proceeds to develop a more general model by introducing an additional exogenous process $\{v_t\}$. He shows that in this more general model p_t is represented by the sum of two discrete linear stochastic processes in both $\{u_t\}$ and $\{v_t\}$ values, hence the rational expectation p_t^* may be expressed in these same values. It is not, in general, possible to reduce this expectation to autoregressive form; rational expectations must be based on past values of either the $\{u_t\}$ or the $\{v_t\}$ process in addition to $\{p_t\}$.

[e]That is, a serially uncorrelated stochastic process, with zero mean and constant variance.

Thus, as soon as a second exogenous variable appears in the system, the rational expectation is no longer an extrapolative expectation. This is in fact the usual situation since the number of component processes making up each endogenous variable will in general be equal to the number of exogenous processes entering the system . . . We may conclude then that under fairly general circumstances: (1) endogenous variables are generated as a sum of linear stochastic processes and (2) because a rational expectation is the expectation of this sum of processes it generally cannot be expressed just in terms of the past history of the particular variable, i.e., it is not an extrapolative expectation. This implies that *serious errors of specification may arise if expectations are actually formed rationally, but in an empirical model they are regarded as functions of past history only . . .* [29]

This result is not limited only to models which *explicitly* assume autoregressive forecasting, but applies to *all* forecasting models which base forecasts only on the past history of the variable being forecast, including "error learning mechanisms."

A corollary of this result is that there is not a simple error-learning rule for adaptive revision of predictions in terms of just the most recent error . . . Consequently, just as errors of specification may arise in empirical work if expectations are assumed to depend on past history alone, they may also arise if it is assumed that the revision of expectations depends only on the error of predicting . . . [30]

These specification errors, then, will be present in models which do not explicitly take account of the structure of the process predicted, if expectations are, in fact, formed rationally. The models of inflation presented in Chapter 4 of this study are used to derive explicit representations of rational expectations of inflation. The results of testing the rational expectations hypothesis under these models are quite favorable to Muth's hypothesis.

Nelson's paper, then, serves two important functions. It gives an explanation for the confusion in the literature between rational expectations and the universally applied autoregressive models, and it shows that these models, in general, may *not* serve as adequate specifciations of rational expectations. This suggests the desirability of (1) further work on models based on broader information subsets than those typically found in the literature and (2) verification of the hypothesis of rational expectations in applied work.

2.2 Extrapolative Models of Inflation Forecasts

This section surveys a body of literature in which expectations of inflation are based solely upon information contained in the history of that series; we shall refer to such models as weak-form[f] hypotheses of forecast formation. We will argue that this body of literature can be traced to Irving Fisher, and can be interpreted as assuming that certain types of information are so costly to collect and process that they are not incorporated by investors into forecasts of inflation, hence are not reflected in market prices. The studies surveyed here are only a small sample of those available in the literature, so pervasive and unquestioned is the use of extrapolative models. I shall not describe these studies in detail. Rather, I shall focus on those aspects that are of interest to the present study.

The first writer to introduce a model of expectations formation explicitly into an analysis of inflationary expectations was Irving Fisher,[32] in *The Theory of Interest*.[g] Fisher was careful to develop the relationship between nominal interest, real interest, and the expected rate of inflation in the context of a model assuming perfect foresight and instantaneous adjustment. Fisher, of course, recognized that the world he lived in was not one of perfect foresight. While he recognized the effect of inflation on the nominal rate of interest, he did not think that the relationship was due to conscious adjustment to expected price changes.

It should be noted that insofar as there exists any adjustment of the money rate of interest to the changes in the purchasing power of money, it is for the most part (1) *lagged* and (2) *indirect*. The lag, distributed, has been shown to extend over several years. The indirectness of the effect of changed purchasing power comes largely through the *intermediate* steps which affect business profits and volumes of trade, which in turn affect the demand for loans and the rate of interest. *There is very little direct and conscious adjustment through foresight.* Where such foresight is conspicuous, as in the final period of German inflation, there is less lag in the effects.[34]

---

[f]The concepts of weak-form, semistrong-form, and strong-form hypotheses of forecast formation were developed by Eugene Fama in a closely related context,[31] that of efficient markets. Heuristically, a market is efficient if the price *fully reflects* a certain subset of available information. The tests which we perform in Chapter 3 test whether a certain market price *reflects* a certain subset of information. This does not, however, imply that the information is fully reflected, i.e., that arbitrage opportunities are absent. I am grateful to B.T. McCallum for this point.

[g]This is not to claim that he was the first to recognize such expectations or their influence on the nominal rate of interest. This influence was recognized by the classical writers. For example, John Stuart Mill states, concerning a depreciation in the value of money:

... depreciation, merely as such, while in the process of taking place, tends to raise the rate of interest: and the expectation of further depreciation adds to this effect; because lenders who expect that their interest will be paid, and the principal perhaps redeemed, in a less valuable currency than they lent, of course required a rate of interest sufficient to cover this contingent loss.[33]

We mean to imply here only that Fisher was the first to apply his model to econometric work, regressing nominal rates of interest on distributed lags of past price changes. I am grateful to Leland B. Yeager for drawing my attention to the passage from Mill's *Principles*.

And again,

How is it possible for a borrower to foresee variations in the general price level with the resultant increase or decrease in the buying power of money? A change in the value of money is hard to determine. Few businessmen have any clear ideas about it. If we ask a merchant whether or not he takes account of appreciation or depreciation on money values he will say he never heard of it, that "a dollar is a dollar!" In his mind, other things may change in terms of money, but money itself does not change. Most people are subject to what may be called the "money illusion," and think instinctively of money as constant and incapable of appreciation or depreciation. Yet it may be true that *they do take account, to some extent at least, even if unconsciously, of a change in the buying power of money*, under guise of a change in the level of prices in general.[35]

Fisher's cautious wording makes it clear that he did not recognize the conscious processing of information in the production of forecasts of inflation. It is no wonder, then, that he did not treat investors as gathering other types of information (e.g., money growth rates, as Marshall and Keynes recognized) than historical price data to produce their forecasts of inflation.

Fisher did recognize, though, that there might be reasons for investors to try to forecast prices:

. . . and today especially, foresight is clearer and more prevalent than ever before. The businessman makes a definite effort to look ahead not only as to his particular business but as to general business conditions, including the trend of prices.[36]

He cited several examples of evidence concerning expectations of inflation and the nominal rate of interest, including the free silver agitation of 1895 and 1896, in California during the inflation period of the Civil War and Gold Rupee bonds on the Indian Exchange from 1875-1892.

. . . the rates realized to investors in bonds of the two different standards differed but slightly until 1875, when the fall of Indian exchange began. The average difference from 1875 to 1892 inclusive was 0.7 percent. Within this period, from 1884 exchange fell much more rapidly than before, and the difference in the two rates of interest rose accordingly, amounting in one year to 1.1 percent. Inasmuch as the two bonds were issued by the same government, possessed the same degree of security, were quoted side by side in the same market, and were similar in all important respects except in the standard in which they are expressed, *the results afford evidence that the fall of exchange (after it once began) was, to some extent, discounted in advance and affected the rates of interest in those standards.* Of course investors did not form perfectly definite estimates of the future fall, but the fear of a fall predominated in varying degrees over the hope of a rise.[37]

Fisher felt that adjustment of interest to changes in the value of money was slow and indirect. He cited evidence of highly variable and frequently negative real rates of interest in support of this thesis. His explanation for this phenomenon was framed, in large part, in terms of money illusion:

When prices begin to rise, money interest is scarcely affected. It requires the cumulative effect of a long rise, or a marked rise in prices, to produce a definite advance in the interest rate. If there were no money illusion and if adjustments of interest rates were perfect, *unhindered by any failure to foresee future* changes in the purchasing power of money or by custom or law or any other impediment, we should have found a very different set of facts.[38]

Fisher maintained that it is this lack of foresight which makes the relation between money rates of interest and real rates interesting:

If the money rate of interest were perfectly adjusted to changes in the purchasing power of money—which means in effect, if those changes were perfectly and universally foreseen—the relation of the rate of interest to those changes would have no practical importance but only a theoretical importance. *As matters are, however, in view of almost universal lack of foresight,* the relation has greater practical than theoretical importance. The businessman supposes he makes his contract in a certain rate of interest, only to wake up later and find that in terms of real goods, the rate is quite different.[39]

Before commenting briefly on Fisher's empirical work in this area, we can sum up his views about the expected rate of inflation: (1) Fisher recognized that in a world of perfect foresight investors would act so as to adjust nominal rates of interest for the expected rate of inflation. (2) He felt that investors were plagued by "money illusion" which destroyed this theoretical relationship. (3) Nevertheless he argued that there will be a strong relation between rates of inflation and the nominal rate of interest which is partly due to foresight as individuals use this information to produce forecasts of inflation, and partly due to a cumulative effect of inflation on profits and the volume of trade.

The empirical evidence gathered by Fisher about the relation between nominal interest and inflation was concerned with both effects under (3) in the above paragraph; and it was precisely the latter effect which Fisher used to explain the extraordinarily long lags which he found. He was *not* primarily concerned with a test of a hypothesis of forecast formation:

Since the theory being investigated is that interest rates move in the opposite direction to changes in the value of money, that is, in the same direction as price changes, the first analysis made is the same as that already made by rougher methods, the comparison of *price changes* with interest rates.[40]

Fisher used quarterly data for Great Britain and the United States to test his hypothesis. He noted that the correlation between concurrent inflation and interest was unimpressive, but notes that the correlation improves markedly when the rate of inflation is lagged 4 years for the U.S. and 6 years for Great Britain. He argues, however, that a distributed lag is more appropriate than a discrete lag:

But a little consideration suggests that the influence of P' or i may be assumed to be distributed in time—as, in fact, must evidently be true of any influence.[41]

Fisher then formed a variable $\overline{P}'$ which is a distributed lag of past rates of inflation, where the weights of the lag distribution are constrained (1) to lie on a straight line, (2) to sum to one, and (3) to decline monotonically to zero at the tail of the lag distribution. The correlation between this variable and nominal rates of interest in the U.S. and U.K. is much higher:

Our first correlations seemed to indicate that the relationship between P' and i is either very slight or obscured by other factors. But when we make the much more reasonable supposition that price changes do not exhaust their effects in a single year but manifest their influence with diminishing intensity, over long periods which vary in length with the conditions, we find a very significant relationship, especially in the period which includes the World War, when prices were subject to violent fluctuations.[42]

However, lags that Fisher found were extremely long;

... for Great Britain in 1898-1924, the highest value of r (+0.980) is reached when effects of price changes are *assumed to be spread over 28 years* or for a weighted average of 9.3 years, while for the United States the highest r (+0.857) is for a distribution of the influence due to price changes over 20 years or a weighted average of 7.3 years.[43]

For commercial paper rates in the United States Fisher found the lag that maximized the correlation coefficient to be "120 quarters or 30 years."[h] It is

---

[h]Laffer and Zecher[44] attempted to reproduce these results using Fisher's data. They regressed the nominal commercial paper rate on a constant and a 120-quarter arithmetic distributed lag of actual inflation and found:

$$i = 2.0132 + 0.8546\overline{P}'_{120} + \qquad \begin{array}{l} R^2 = 0.558 \\ F = 37.81 \\ DW = 0.313 \end{array}$$
$$\quad (4.03) \quad (6.15)$$

which almost duplicate Fisher's result. They point to the low Durbin-Watson statistic which "provides sufficient grounds to question these results."[45] After estimating the equation with no constraint on the lag distribution they find the coefficients more or less evenly distributed, some positive, some negative, and the sum of the coefficients is −0.036, not even positive. This provides "tentative disconfirmation of the hypothesis."[46]

important to understand that Fisher interpreted these estimated lags in terms of the total effect of inflation on interest, *not* as an estimate of the lag in the formation of forecasts of inflation by investors:

It seems fantastic, at first glance, to ascribe to events which occurred last century any influence affecting the rate of interest today. And yet that is what the correlations with distributed effects of P' show. A little thought should convince the reader that the effects of bumper wheat crops, revolutionary discoveries and inventions, Japanese earthquakes, Mississippi floods, and similar events project their influence upon prices and interest rates over many future years *even after the original causal event has been forgotten.* The skeptical reader need only be reminded that the economic effects on the farmer of the deflation of 1920, are now, in 1929, sufficiently acute to make farm relief a pressing political problem and that these economic effects may be expected to persist for many years to come. A further probable explanation of the surprising length of time by which the rate of interest lags behind price changes is that between price changes and interest rates a *third factor intervenes.* This is *business*, as exemplified or measured by the volume of trade. *It is influenced by price changes and influences in turn the rate of interest.*[47]

In my judgment, Fisher has been seriously misinterpreted by many modern writers on expectations mechanisms. These writers have interpreted Fisher's empirical work as showing the relation between past inflation and expected inflation, and the long lags as evidence of a slowness to incorporate new information into forecasts.[i] In contrast we have argued that this is not the main point of Fisher's analysis. He was interested in the total relation between inflation and interest, which, he argued, is based upon many effects additional to those of expected inflation. The body of recent literature using weak-form hypotheses about the formation of expectations of inflation is, in large part, similar in form to the relationship estimated by Fisher. They are commonly interpreted today, however, as yielding estimates of the way in which individuals form forecasts, a meaning entirely different than that suggested by Irving Fisher.

Phillip Cagan[49] was one of the earliest modern authors to develop a weak-form model of expectations of inflation. He hypothesized that the demand for money (in a hyperinflation) is inversely related to the expected inflation rate, and he chose an "adaptive expectations" model for forecast formation. In a discrete model this can be formalized as:

$$\pi_t^* - \pi_{t-1}^* = (1 - \beta)[\pi_{t-1} - \pi_{t-1}^*] \tag{2.4}$$

---

[i]Friedman, for example, remarked:

... Let the higher rate of monetary growth produce rising prices, and let the public *come to expect* that prices will continue to rise. Borrowers will then be willing to pay, and lenders will then demand higher interest rates ... as Irving Fisher pointed out decades ago. This price expectations effect is slow to develop and slow to disappear. Fisher estimated that it took several decades for a full adjustment and more recent work is consistent with his estimates.[48]

where β is a constant, π_t^* is the rate of inflation expected during period t on the basis of information available in period $t-1$, and π_{t-1} is the realized rate of inflation during period $t-1$, which is known to the forecaster at the time he makes his forecast for period t. This rule simply states that the investor will alter his forecast for next period, by a fraction of the error he made this period. That this is a weak-form hypothesis can immediately be seen from:

$$\pi_t^* + (1 - \beta - 1)\pi_{t-1}^* = (1 - \beta)\pi_{t-1},$$

$$\pi_t^* \, (1 - \beta L) = (1 - \beta)\pi_{t-1},$$

$$\pi_t^* = \frac{(1 - \beta)}{(1 - \beta L)}\pi_{t-1}, \tag{2.5}$$

where L is the "Lag Operator" defined such that $Lx_t = x_{t-1}$. The resultant expression (2.5) shows that the expected rate of inflation in this model is represented by a geometric distributed lag in past actual rates of inflation with parameter β. Cagan's use of (2.5) in demand for money equations for seven hyperinflations was apparently judged very successful, and led to the adoption of similar adaptive expectations schemes by other writers, e.g., Friedman.[50] Even though Cagan felt that his surrogate for expectations performed well in his tests, he recognized that there could be other factors influencing expectations.

In the light of the sharp rise of the balances when a reform in the currency approaches, any diminution in the rate at which notes were issued would likely alter the prevailing expectation of a certain rate of future inflation to one of a less rapid rate ... the precise timing of such shifts in expectations appears *incapable of prediction by economic variables*, even though we may be certain such shifts will eventually occur under the circumstances.[51]

Most writers since Cagan have agreed that weak-form hypotheses are sufficient for empirical purposes and have devoted little effort to examining alternative expectations mechanisms.

Other writers who have employed weak-form or extrapolative hypotheses of forecast formation include Ball,[52] Roll,[53] Gibson,[54] Sargent,[55] Siebke-Willms,[56] Andersen-Carlson,[57] Feldstein-Eckstein,[58] Yohe-Karnosky,[59] Gordon,[60] Turnovsky,[61] and Modigliani-Schiller.[62] Other uses of this forecasting mechanism include: (1) market price expectations, Muth[63] and Nerlove;[64] (2) income expectations, Friedman[65] and Zellner, Huang, and Chau;[66] (3) interest rate expectations, Modigliani-Schiller,[67] Grilliches and Wallace,[68] Modigliani-Schiller,[69] and Nelson.[70] In addition autoregressive forecasts are incorporated in most existing macromodels, including the FRB-MIT model[71] and the St. Louis model.[72] The particular forms of the expectations mechanisms differ widely; we find static expectations, error-learning models, adaptive expectations, and extrapolative expectations. Distributed lags of all varieties are used: arithmetic, geometric, Pascal, and Almon polynomial. The important point, however, is that each model is a special case of the general category of weak-form hypotheses about the formation of forecasts. The possibility that market traders may find it to their advantage to gather other types of information to increase the accuracy of their forecasts is seldom explored.

It may be worth illustrating the widespread acceptance of weak-form hypotheses of forecast formation and the confusion between rational expectations and the weak-form models typically used in their stead by considering a few examples of recent views on expectation mechanisms. David Laidler in a recent discussion of Phillips curve studies remarked:

There is a good deal of evidence to support the view that price expectations are on the whole largely based on past experience.[73]

Unfortunately Laidler did not bother to cite any studies in which such evidence can be found. To be sure, models in which expectations are based largely on past experience have been estimated and have often yielded valuable explanatory power for interest rates, unemployment, and the demand for money. However, to my knowledge, there has been no study before this one in which the usual weak-form hypotheses have been tested against a more explicit model of rational or consistent expectations.

Similar testimony to the tacit acceptance of autoregressive forecasting is found in Roll's comment on the importance of properly timing the variables in expectations models:

At this point the importance of timing different variables should be emphasized. For the Gibson Paradox relation there is no theoretical reason for not using interest rates and price levels of the same calendar dates even though they become publicly available at different times. No predictive relation in either relation is necessarily implied and as long as the fitted equation is not regarded as predictively useful but only as a description of simultaneous economic events, no harm is done by disregarding the information lag. This is also true of included variables such as those related to national income and to the money stock. Much more care is warranted in the case of the *anticipated inflation rate, which is always measured as a function of past rates.* If anticipations are presumed to be formed on the basis of those past rates, one must be sure they are observable at least by the date when interest rates are observed.[74]

Roll's point concerning the information lag is, indeed, well taken. His reference to "included variables" will serve to illustrate an important point. Several writers, e.g., Sargent,[75] Ball,[76] Yoke-Karnosky,[77] Feldstein-Eckstein,[78] Tuttle-Wilbur,[79] have included monetary variables in their regressions of nominal rates of interest on past price changes. The variables included have typically been *concurrent* measures of the real money stock or real monetary base, or their percentage rates of change, all of which are useless as expectations variables. They are included to capture the "liquidity" effect of money on interest, in order that the authors may get a better picture of what they regard as the *true* expectations variables, past rates of change of price.

Finally, Foley and Sidrauski provide further evidence of the unquestioned acceptance of extrapolative forecasting mechanisms in both theoretical and empirical work when they state:

> ... the expected capital gains or losses of each of the assets presumably depend on the behavior of the price of capital and the price of money in the past, *as well as on how people extrapolate past behavior into the future.*[80]

Evidence of the confusion between rational expectations and weak-form hypotheses (which we argued is due to Muth's choice of an example to illustrate rational expectations) is adequately given by the following passage from Nelson:

> ... Turnovsky recently proposed that a test of unbiasedness in business economists is at the same time a test of the rationality of these predictions. Turnovsky also stated that in the 'general case' where expectations are formed according to an autoregressive scheme, that autoregressive scheme must be the same one which generates the realizations ... Similarly, Sargent defined the rational expectation of future spot interest rates to be the optimal linear extrapolation of past spot rates for purposes of testing the expectations theory of the term structure of interest rates.[81]

I would like to touch briefly upon one further point relating to autoregressive models before closing this discussion: the tendency to think of expectations of inflation as subject only to slow and minor adjustments in the face of new information; i.e., the predominant belief in *long lags.* As mentioned above, Fisher found lags ranging from twenty to thirty years, with average lags usually around ten years. As we argued above, Fisher did not intend these estimates to refer to the length of time taken to form forecasts; however, work since that time has interpreted this measure in the manner of Cagan, as the lag in forming expectations. This specification error—if forecasts are actually formed rationally—has been responsible for much misinterpretation of observed interest rates. Hendershott and Horwich, for example, refer to the estimates of long lags found by Gibson and Sargent:

> ... Their experience contradicts the monetary voices in government, industry and the academy that proclaim, but do not demonstrate, that price level expectations, rather than real forces, are largely responsible for interest rate movements in this decade.[82]

Long lags have been found for short rates of interest. This led Friedman and Schwartz to make the rather paradoxical statement:

The rate of interest is a forward-looking price connected with economic transactions involving the most far-sighted and long-lived considerations—the savings and investment process or the accumulation and maintenance of wealth. *This is true even for short-term interest rates,* in the sense that the funds being made available for lending at short-term are generally part of a total stock of wealth accumulated for long-term purposes; it just happens to be prudent or profitable to make this part of wealth available to others for short periods at a time; and corresponding statements apply to the funds borrowed at short-term. *Hence, it is reasonable that participants in this market should be taking a fairly long view, forming fairly firm opinions and altering them only gradually rather than permitting their anticipations to alter substantially with every momentary change of circumstances.* [83]

As we shall see in the next chapter, decisions about what types of information to collect and process into forecasts and of the volatility of expectations of inflation depend on costs and rewards to accurate forecasting, not on metaphysical explanations of the short-term bond market.

Sargent notes:

... the result (of regressing nominal interest on past prices) ... has been to produce estimates of extraordinarily long distributed lags, lags that have been imputed to a tendency of the public to form its expectations of inflation with a very long lag. Yet the average lags are so long, typically ranging between ten and thirty years, that their credibility as estimates of lags in forming expectations has often been sharply questioned. [84]

Although more recent writers—e.g., Yohe-Karnosky[85]—have found shorter lags for the U.S. during the past two decades, there still seems to be much sentiment for the existence of long lags. We maintain that these long lags are the result of the specification error implicit in all weak-form hypotheses of expectation formation since they exclude the influence of other variables which are used by investors in forming forecasts of inflation. We will present evidence in the next chapter that the lags involved are far shorter than typically believed and do not result from a hesitancy of investors to use new information, but rather from the inherent lag in the structure of the economy between changes in money growth rates and changes in the rate of inflation.

In all fairness, I must conclude with a disclaimer. I do not wish to suggest that all economists have ignored the effect of alternative types of information on forecasts of inflation. However, this recognition has, as yet, not been incorporated into empirical work. Evidence of understanding of more sophisticated expectations schemes is easily uncovered in the recent expectations literature. Soltow and Luckett state:

. . . What appears to have gone largely unappreciated is the possibility that monetary/debt management policy may be able to influence the term structure indirectly by altering investors' expectations.[86]

Brunner and Meltzer note:

Evidence of the revived interest (in monetary theory) is the much greater attention now given by economists, politicians, speculators and even journalists to changes in the stock of money and its growth rate.[87]

Foley and Sidrauski hint at rational forecasts when they write:

. . . In addition, expectations about future price changes may also depend on the behavior of the government itself. A change in government behavior may induce people to believe that the government has changed its policy goals and may result in a change of the private sector's expectations about future price behavior.[88]

There is also evidence, although sparse, that more sophisticated models of forecast formation have been incorporated into empirical work. Turnovsky writes:

The expectations equations we have been discussing all assume that forecasts of future price changes are obtained from past price movements alone. They can therefore be described as purely autoregressive. While all the usual expectations make this assumption, which in the final analysis may be supported by empirical evidence, it is nevertheless important to examine the possibility that price forecasts depend on other variables as well. After all, people have access to a variety of information related to other economic variables which they are likely to influence price expectations is some notion of the current level of economic activity.[89]

Turnovsky then proceeded to introduce the unemployment rate into an interest rate equation to capture more of the expectations of inflation than with a purely autoregressive scheme. It seems, though, that Turnovsky was unaware of the link between this effort and rational expectations because (1) he made no effort to specify a structure generating inflation to help him pick the additional variables used in forecasting and (2) in the next section he proposed a test of rationality which is essentially a test of the unbiasedness of business economists' reported predictions.

Andersen and Carlson reported estimates of an equation in the Appendix to their model on "Alternative Price Equations:"

. . . The second alternative (the first was using a market interest rate as a proxy for expectations of inflation) that is considered is based on the central proposition of the quantity theory—that changes in money are ultimately reflected in changes in the price level. Accordingly, current and past changes in money are used as a proxy to measure anticipated movements in prices. Though this rationale for including money is somewhat narrower than that proposed by some monetary economists, the direct and indirect effects of money are being measured once it is included in the price equation.[90]

Several comments are in order. (1) They did not provide a rationale for including money growth, and they did not suggest any link between their equation and rational expectations. (2) If they had examined rational expectations in more detail, they would probably have been led to include *both* past histories of prices and of money, as we do in the next two chapters. (3) They include the current rate of change in the money supply, which is useless to investors, because it is not available at the time of the forecast—further evidence that the authors were not thinking of a conscious forecasting mechanism on the part of market traders.

I will examine several of the conclusions of these papers, as well as others, in the course of the next four chapters. In many cases the empirical conclusions regarding length of lag and level of sophitication of market forecasts will be quite different from those usually found in the body of literature employing weak-form forecasts. We will argue that this is due, in part, to errors in specification in all models which try to estimate expectations while omitting variables regarded as important in forecasting by investors. The models of Consistent and Rational Expectations which we estimate as alternatives to weak-form hypotheses are, I maintain, less guilty of such errors in specification. Our tests will show that these semistrong-form hypotheses of forecast formation are, in general, more efficient than weak-form hypotheses—precisely why they are adopted by investors in the market.

3   Optimal Use of Information

In economics, the unifying core of theory is the axiom of rational self-interest; belief in the relevance of this axiom is the science's *sine qua non*.[1]

In previous chapters I have contended that the large class of hypotheses of expectations of inflation typically used in the literature, i.e., weak-form hypotheses, are not well-grounded in choice-theoretic models of investor behavior. They are usually justified by positing some reasonable mechanism by which forecasts are generated, or by which forecasts are altered, such as adaptive expectations, extrapolative expectations, or an error-learning process. The common feature of these models is that resulting predictions of the rate of inflation are autoregressive; the subset of available information incorporated into forecasts is confined to past values of the rate of inflation. Since there exist many other sources of information about future inflation (consider, for example, any econometric model of the macroeconomy), it is possible that these sources are also used by investors in making predictions. The sources actually exploited will depend on costs of collection and gains in predictive accuracy. Indeed, it is not difficult to imagine a set of information costs which would induce investors to only forecast extrapolatively. I maintain, however, that this is an issue which deserves explicit testing.

The object of this chapter is to present a formal analysis of the problem faced by an investor, in a world of certainty, who must choose the amount of information to collect and process, when collection of information is costly, and increased information increases the percentage yield of the investor's portfolio. We will specify the costs and returns to information processing in a general way, and analyze the conditions for optimality, noting implications for cooperation and economies of scale.

Once we have looked at the formal problem faced by the investor, we will be interested in testing the applicability of autoregressive expectations to the real world. In other words, we would like to ascertain whether or not costs and returns to exploiting alternative sources of information are such that they are reflected in market prices. This means we would like to test the hypothesis of autoregressive expectations against an alternative hypothesis, based on a weaker assumption about other sources of information, which we shall call consistent expectations. We will present a model of inflation, in which the rate of inflation is assumed to be determined by distributed lags in (1) rates of change of the supply of money and (2) rates of change in government expenditures. Under fairly general assumptions this model can be reduced to a model in which the optimal prediction of inflation is based on available information about (1) past rates of inflation and (2) past rates of change in the supply of money. Consistent expectations, then, is the hypothesis that the market prediction of inflation reflects information contained in the past history of money growth *in addition to* information contained in the past history of the rate of inflation. Rejection of the hypothesis of autoregressive expectations in favor of the alternative hypothesis of consistent expectations will serve as evidence of an error in specifciation of models employing autoregressive forecasting mechanisms, and will throw into serious question tests of any hypotheses which have been carried out in the context of autoregressive predictions. The point of this test is to present evidence that the subset of available information reflected in autoregressive expectations is too limiting to represent investor behavior. I will not claim to have identified all sources of information exploited, nor to have shown—at this point—that the additional information is used in a way consistent with the structure of the economy.

We shall follow most writers in assuming the validity of the Fisher relation, which asserts that expectations of inflation are reflected in nominal rates of interest. The introduction of rates of change in the money supply forces us to explicitly consider the liquidity effect, and to propose an alternative nominal rate of interest implied by existing market rates, which we expect will be less sensitive to the liquidity effect than market spot rates. In particular, we shall employ an *implicit forward rate of interest*, calculated under the assumption of the "unbiased expectations" theory of the term structure of interest rates. The test will also be carried out with various spot rates of interest as a comparison. The results are uniformly in support of the hypothesis of consistent expectations, indicating that the extreme assumptions concerning information costs are not, at least in the case of information on money growth rates, justified.

Later in this chapter, a related issue will be examined under the hypothesis of consistent expectations. A number of authors have estimated the lag in the formation of expectations of inflation to be extremely long. Our model, on the other hand, implies that this lag should roughly correspond to the lag implicit in the structure of the process generating actual inflation. Examination of the empirical results indicates that this is, in fact, the case. An explanation for the spuriously long lags found in other studies is advanced.

3.1 Optimal Use of Information

We will now examine a model of investor behavior in which various types of information are related to a measure of value to the forecaster via a production function. Consider an investor in the context of a two-period utility maximization problem. Our investor faces given incomes, y_1 in period 1 and y_2 in period 2, given initial assets a_1, and a given rate of interest r_0 that can be earned on investments without gathering information. The investor also has the opportunity to gather information to increase the percentage return of his portfolio, but must pay the costs of collecting and processing such information. We treat the problem of choice as choosing the level of consumption in period one, c_1, the size of the portfolio invested until period two, a_2, and the optimal amount of information to process so as to maximize the utility index, $U = U(c_1, c_2)$.

To preserve generality, we would identify each source of information I_1, $I_2, \ldots, I_n$ and specify a production function $f(I_1 \ldots, I_n)$ indicating the increase in percent return on the investment over the market return, r_0, due to information processing as a function of those inputs of information. Then, given the costs of collection, we would define the expansion path of forecast return in terms of the inputs.

It will greatly simplify our analysis, however, if we are able to treat the forecast production process in two stages: (1) choose the optimal combinations of inputs given alternative levels of total outlay in the production of forecasts and (2) choose the optimal level of the forecasting activity in terms of total outlay on forecasting. In Figure 3-1 f_1, f_2, f_3 represent isoreturn loci; e.g., combinations of I_i and I_j on f_1 yield the same increase over r_0 in the percent return to the investment, and $f_3 > f_2 > f_1$. $S_1, S_2,$ and S_3 represent loci of

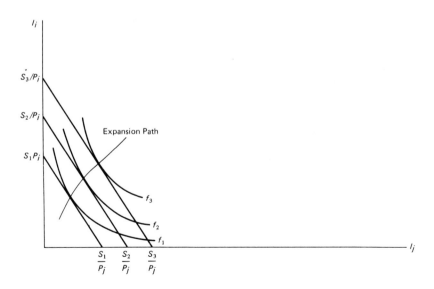

Figure 3-1. Optimal Combinations of Information Inputs.

constant expenditure on information, with $S_3 > S_2 > S_1$, and are drawn under the assumption of constant unit costs of processing each source of information. If we make the equivalent to the nonsatiety axiom in consumer theory we can define a unique value of $f(I_1, \ldots I_n)$ associated with each level of total outlay $S_i = P_1 I_1^* + \ldots + P_n I_n^*$, where the starred values of the I's indicate that they correspond to points of tangency with isoexpenditure curves. We find it convenient to define, then, $f(S)$ relating (maximum) increases in percent return to the investment for given levels of outlay; clearly $f(S)$ is well defined and $d(f[S])/dS > 0$. S, then, refers to total dollar outlay on forecasting activities, and assumes a prior maximization process. This analysis assumes that relative prices of sources of information are given to the investor; if they change, then the properties of $f(S)$ will also change.

We are now in a position to state the problem facing the investor more directly. The investor will choose the value of c_1 and S so as to

$$\max_{c_1, S} \quad U(c_1, c_2) \tag{3.1}$$

subject to

$$c_2 = y_2 + a_2$$

And once we recognize that $a_2 = (y_1 + a_1 - c_1 - S)(1 + r_0 + f[S])$ we find the solution in the familiar way.

$$\max L = U(c_1, c_2) - \lambda[c_2 - y_2 - (y_1 + a_1 - c_1 - S)(1 + r_0 + f[S])] \tag{3.2}$$

$$\partial L/\partial c_1 = \partial U/\partial c_1 - \lambda(1 + r_0 - f[S]), \tag{3.3}$$

$$\partial L/\partial c_2 = \partial U/\partial c_2 - \lambda, \tag{3.4}$$

$$\partial L/\partial S = -\lambda[(1 + r_0 + f[S]) - (y_1 + a_1 - c_1 - S)f'(S)], \tag{3.5}$$

$$\partial L/\partial \lambda = [c_2 - y_2 - (y_1 + a_1 - c_1 - S)(1 + r_0 + f[S])](-1), \tag{3.6}$$

Setting (3.3) through (3.6) equal to zero we get the following first-order conditions for an internal solution. (3.3) and (3.4) yield

$$MU_1/MU_2 = 1 + r_0 + f(S), \tag{3.7}$$

and from (3.5) we see that the first-order condition for optimal production of forecasts is

$$1 + r_0 + f(S) = (y_1 + a_1 - c_1 - S)f'(S) = MU_1/MU_2. \tag{3.8}$$

The second equality in (3.8) tells us that optimal forecasting requires that the rate at which the investor can trade off future for present consumption via forecasting be equal to the rate at which he is indifferent to doing so.

An interesting feature of this solution is worth pointing out. Given a level of outlay on forecasting S_0, the marginal return to forecasting, $MR = f'(S)(y_1 + a_1 - c_1 - S)$, varies proportionately with the size of the portfolio $P = y_1 + a_1 - c_1 - S$. That is, $\partial MR / \partial P = f'(S_0) > 0$, a positive constant. In Figure 3-2, as long as $f'(S) > 0$ there always exists a size of portfolio P^* large enough that it will pay the investor to make the S_0 dollar outlay on information processing. The reader's first reaction might be to suppose that only large investors will produce forecasts employing large amounts of S. If transactions costs are not prohibitive, though, it will prove valuable for investors to pool their portfolios, or, equivalently, to produce cooperative forecasts.

If transactions costs were zero, investors would group together to produce forecasts. Given any level of outlay S_0, there exists a total size of portfolio, hence a total number of cooperative investors, such that $MR > MC$. Sources of information will be exploited until $f'(S)$ goes to zero.

In the real world, of course, transactions costs are not zero; thus $f'(S)$ will not fall to zero. Our main point, however, has been made. There are incentives for investors to join together to produce forecasts, implying a much more thorough exploitation of information than would take place if individual investors were forced to act alone. Mutual funds and other cooperative investment facilities may well be observable consequences of such economies of

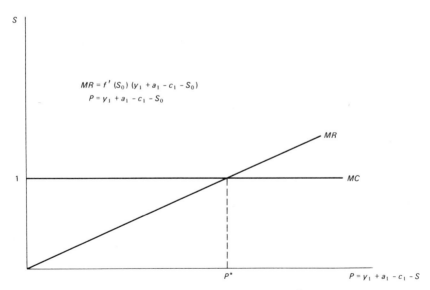

Figure 3-2. Marginal Costs and Returns to Information.

scale in the production of forecasts. Other examples are the services of securities analysts and professional brokers, making centrally processed forecasts for large groups of individual investors who jointly pay the cost of collection and processing.

3.2 Estimating Inflationary Expectations

Before we can test alternative hypotheses about the formation of unobservable expectations of inflation, we must develop a proxy measure for them. Most previous work has recognized that in equilibrium the nominal rate of interest must approximately equal the real rate of interest plus the expected rate of inflation, all defined over the same time period,

$$r_t = \rho_t + \pi_t^*. \tag{3.9}$$

We would like to be able to estimate relationships like

$$\pi_t^* = h(Z) + a_0, \tag{3.10}$$

where Z represents all past values of the variables which are hypothesized to be important for forecast formation and $h(\cdot)$ stands for the particular functional (weighted average) of these values which best explains π_t^*. The hypothesis of consistent expectations implies that market traders have found it worth their while to learn about the structure of the process generating inflation in the economy and to gather information on the variables which appear in that process. We will present a simple model of the process which generates inflation and examine how an investor with knowledge of that process would forecast the rate of inflation.

Let the rate of inflation, a stochastic process, be represented by the reduced form Equation (3.11) from a suitably chosen structural model,

$$\pi_t = \theta X_t + \gamma Y_t + a_0. \tag{3.11}$$

Inflation, in this model, is a weighted sum of two stochastic processes X_t and Y_t; γ and θ are the reduced-form multipliers, combinations of the parameters of the structural model from which (3.11) was derived. The exogenous variables X_t and Y_t are driven, respectively, by the stochastic processes $\{m_t\}$ and $\{v_t\}$. Thus we have

$$X_t = m_t + \phi_1 m_{t-1} + \ldots + \phi_q m_{t-q} \tag{3.12}$$

$$= (1 + \phi_1 L + \ldots + \phi_q L^q) m_t = \phi(L) m_t,$$

$$Y_t = v_t + \xi_1 v_{t-1} + \ldots + \xi_p v_{t-p} \tag{3.13}$$

$$= (1 + \xi_1 L + \ldots + \xi_p L^p) v_t = \xi(L) v_t,$$

where L is the lag operator defined such that $Lm_t = m_{t-1}$. Both $\{m_t\}$ and $\{v_t\}$ are "white noise," i.e., serially uncorrelated stochastic processes with zero mean and constant variance. Past realizations of both processes—i.e., values prior to $t-1$—are predetermined at the beginning of period t, hence have zero variance. X_t and Y_t are the realizations of passing the white noise processes $\{m_t\}$ and $\{v_t\}$, respectively, through the linear filters $\phi(L)$ and $\xi(L)$, and can be regarded as distributed lags in the processes $\{m_t\}$ and $\{v_t\}$.

In our model[a] m_t will represent the percent rate of change in the stock of money in period t; hence X_t stands for a distributed lag of past money growth rates of (finite) order q. We can let v_t represent some other exogenous variable, or some linear combination of other exogenous variables. For reasons which will become apparent, we can leave some flexibility in its specification.

We can represent the rate of inflation in this model by the reduced form Equation (3.11) after making the substitutions in (3.12) and (3.13):

$$\pi_t = \theta \phi(L) m_t + \gamma \xi(L) v_t + a_0. \tag{3.14}$$

If we assume that the roots of $\xi(L)$ lie *outside* the unit circle[b] then $\xi(L)$ has an inverse and we can write

$$\xi^{-1}(L) \pi_t = \theta \xi^{-1}(L) \phi(L) m_t + \gamma v_t + a_1, \tag{3.15}$$

which expresses π_t as a mixed autoregressive moving average process,

---

[a]The structural model from which (3.11) was derived is discussed in Chapter 4, Section 4.2.

[b]This is the invertibility condition given by Nelson.[2] We can illustrate this invertibility condition with a simple example. Let Z_t be a moving average process of order one in the white noise process $\{u_t\}$, i.e.,

$$Z_t = u_t - \lambda_1 u_{t-1} = (1 - \lambda_1 L) u_t = \lambda(L) u_t.$$

This is equivalent to

$$Z_t + \lambda_1 Z_{t-1} + \lambda_1^2 Z_{t-2} + \ldots = u_t$$

or that

$$Z_t = (-\lambda_1 - \lambda_1^2 L - \ldots) Z_{t-1} + u_t.$$

Nelson states "If Z_t is not to depend increasingly on more distant past Z_{t-k} ... we require that $|\lambda_1| < 1$".[3] This implies that the latent root of $\lambda(L) = 1 - \lambda L$ be strictly greater than one. The analog for moving average processes of order greater than one is that all roots of $\lambda(L)$ lie outside the unit circle.

$$\pi_t = \delta(L)\pi_{t-1} + \theta\xi^{-1}(L)\phi(L)m_t + \gamma v_t + a_1.$$ (3.16)

An investor who knew the process by which inflation is generated could use (3.16) to forecast inflation. At the beginning of period t, $E(m_t) = 0$ and $E(v_t) = 0$, so he will forecast inflation by,

$$\pi_t^* = \delta(L)\pi_{t-1} + \psi(L)m_{t-1} + a_1,$$ (3.17)

where, for convenience, we have substituted $\psi(L) = \theta\xi^{-1}(L)\phi(L)$. Our hypothesis of consistent expectations, then, implies that forecasts of inflation will be made on the basis of the past behavior of the rate of inflation and the past history of money growth rates.

I will test the hypothesis of consistent expectations, (CE), against the alternative hypothesis of autoregressive expectations, (AE), the general class of hypotheses which maintain that forecasts are based solely on the past history of inflation. Most expectations models used in the existing empirical work[4] are of this variety including static expectations, adaptive expectations, extrapolative expectations, and error-learning mechanisms. Formally we may represent AE as an autoregressive process of order p,

$$\pi_t^* = \tau(L)\pi_{t-1} + a_1.$$ (3.18)

We now substitute (3.10) into (3.9) to obtain

$$r_t = h(Z) + \rho_t + a_0.$$ (3.19)

Once we decide how to treat p we can proceed to estimate (3.19) directly by substituting the appropriate form of $h(Z)$ for each hypothesis. One widely used assumption is that we can safely regard the real rate of interest as a constant. To quote Friedman,

It seems entirely satisfactory to take the anticipated real interest rate . . . as fixed for the demand for money. There the real interest rate is at best a supporting actor. Inflation and deflation are surely center stage. Suppressing the variations in the real interest rate (or the deviations of the measured real rate from the anticipated real rate) is unlikely to introduce serious error.[5]

Alternatively we could treat the real rate as a function of a small number of observable variables, and estimate (3.19) directly. Regardless of the particular choice of expectations hypothesis, however, or of the way in which the real rate is treated, the unifying feature of almost all previously published work is the use of a nominal spot rate of interest as the dependent variable in regression equations like (3.19).

The tests presented in this study are not confined to using a nominal spot rate of interest for the dependent variable. The usual procedure is not well suited to testing the hypotheses which interest us. A change in money growth rates will not only alter forecasts of inflation, but will also have a transitory effect on the real rate of interest; this is known as the Liquidity Effect. An alternative rate of interest will be developed in which the real rate has been purged—at least in part—of its dependence on money growth. Our new dependent variable will, furthermore, give insights into some interesting problems concerning the term-to-maturity structure of interest rates.

First, however, a few comments on maintained hypotheses are appropriate. The dependent variable which I will develop is a forward rate of interest which is implied by the term-to-maturity structure of interest rates at a point in time. It takes the purest form of the expectations theory of the term structure of interest rates as given. More specifically it presumes that a spot "force of interest" is equal to the unbiased geometric mean of the consecutive one-period forces of interest which are expected to prevail in the future.[6] I fully recognize that this is the purest form of the theory and that there has been a great deal of work done trying to incorporate liquidity premia and risk premia into the theory and to adjust the theory for factors of debt-management. For simplicity in calculation, however, I neglect all these considerations. This does not mean that I deny their importance to some issues, only that they are viewed as being orthogonal to all explanatory variables in our analysis. The use of a maintained hypothesis should not be based, in any event, on its realism, but on the predictive power that the hypothesis yields. Test results indicate that in this case the hypothesis is quite effective.

3.3 Implicit Forward Rates of Interest

Consider an investor who has decided to loan a sum of money for ten years. The investor faces a wide variety of options; he can buy a ten year bond and hold it until maturity; he can buy a twenty year bond with the anticipation of selling it after ten years; he can buy a five year bond with the intention of reinvesting the proceeds in a similar instrument upon maturity; or he can buy a twenty year bond which has ten remaining years until maturity. Abstracting from risk and liquidity considerations the investor will choose the way to package the investment which yields the highest return. But if all investors consider alternative packages for the same investment as perfect substitutes, then competitive equilibrium will require the yields on alternatively packaged invest-ments to be equal. In particular it must be true that the yield on an $(n+1)$-period bond is, in equilibrium, equal to the expected yield from investing in $n+1$ consecutive one-period bonds. Thus we have

$$(1 + R_{t+n})^{n+1} = (1 + R_t)(1 + r_{t+1}) \ldots (1 + r_{t+n}), \tag{3.20}$$

where R_{t+n} is the $(n + 1)$-period spot rate of interest and r_{t+n} is the anticipated yield on a one-period bond which matures in period n, etc. But this is also true for an n-period bond,

$$(1 + R_{t+n-1})^n = (1 + R_t)(1 + r_{t+1}) \ldots (1 + r_{t+n-1}). \tag{3.21}$$

By combining (3.20) and (3.21) we can compute the anticipated one-period rate of interest for period $(t + n)$.

Thus, we have

$$\frac{(1 + R_{t+n})^{n+1}}{(1 + R_{t+n-1})^n} = (1 + r_{t+n}),$$

which implies

$$r_{t+n} = \frac{(1 + R_{t+n})^{n+1}}{(1 + R_{t+n-1})^n} - 1.0. \tag{3.22}$$

This variable is a forward rate of interest which is implicit in the prices of today's spot market. Under the assumption of the expectations theory of the term-to-maturity structure of interest rates, it is the anticipated one-period rate of interest in period n, the rate which must prevail in the minds of investors to preclude intertemporal arbitrage, i.e., for equilibrium in the bond market.

Because r_{t+n} is a *future* one-period yield I expect that it will not be altered by a transitory influence on short term interest rates. In particular, there is no reason, I assume, for traders to alter their predictions about future short rates because they witness a dip in current rates due to an unanticipated increase in the money supply, the liquidity effect.

The Fisher relation, (3.9), although usually stated in terms of a spot rate of interest, generalizes in a straightforward manner to implicit forward rates of interest,

$$r_{t+n} = \rho_{t+n} + \pi^*_{t+n}. \tag{3.23}$$

Here care must be taken to define all variables over the same period.

The empirical work presented in this chapter is for $n = 1$ in (3.23), i.e., the relevant expected rate of inflation is π^*_{t+1}. I will now derive the expressions for π^*_{t+1} for the hypotheses of CE and AE as presented, respectively, in (3.17) and (3.18).

Define the linear operator F, such that, $Fx_t = x_{t+1}$. Operating on (3.17) by F yields

$$\pi_{t+1}^* = \delta(L)\pi_t + \psi(L)m_t + a_1$$

$$= \delta_0\pi_t + (\delta_1 + \delta_2 L + \ldots + \delta_s L^{s-1})\pi_{t-1} \tag{3.24}$$

$$+ \psi_0 m_t + (\psi_1 + \psi_2 L + \ldots + \psi_q L^{q-1})m_{t-1} + a_1.$$

Now apply a principle developed by Wold[7] known as the "chain principle of forecasting" and replace all the variables on the r.h.s. of (3.24) by their expected values,

$$\pi_{t+1}^* = \delta_0\pi_t^* + \delta'(L)\pi_{t-1} + \psi'(L)m_{t-1} + a_1. \tag{3.25}$$

Replace π_t^* with the equivalent expression (3.17) to get

$$\pi_{t+1}^* = \delta_1(L)\pi_{t-1} + \psi_1(L)m_{t-1} + a_1, \tag{3.26}$$

where the coefficients of $\delta(L)$, $(\delta_0, \delta_1, \ldots, \delta_s)$, determine the coefficients of $\delta_1(L)$, $(\delta_1 + \delta_0^2, \delta_2 + \delta_0\delta_1, \ldots, \delta_s + \delta_0\delta_{s-1}, \delta_0\delta_s)$, in the obvious way.

Thus the hypothesis of CE results in the expression (3.26) for π_{t+1}^* that is based on past realized rates of inflation and past rates of money growth.

Similarly, by operating on (3.18) by F, applying Wold's chain principle of forecasting, and combining terms it is clear that one could derive a similar expression for π_{t+1}^* from the hypothesis of AE;

$$\pi_{t+1}^* = \tau_1(L)\pi_{t-1} + a_2. \tag{3.27}$$

The hypotheses of CE and AE can be tested by substituting, respectively, (3.26) and (3.27) into (3.23), for $n = 1$. The first substitution yields

$$r_{t+1} = \rho_{t+1} + a_1 + \delta_1(L)\pi_{t-1} + \psi_1(L)m_{t-1}. \tag{3.28}$$

The second substitution yields

$$r_{t+1} = \rho_{t+1} + a_2 + \tau_1(L)\pi_{t-1}, \tag{3.29}$$

which is equivalent to (3.28) if $\psi_1(L) = 0$, if all of the coefficients in this lag polynomial are zero. A test of AE against the alternative hypothesis of CE is performed by estimating (3.28); if $\psi_1(L)$ is found to be significantly different from zero, then AE must be rejected in favor of CE.

The dependent variable in (3.28) is a forward interest rate rather than the spot rate used exclusively in the literature. The chief virtue is that it is less sensitive than a spot rate to any effects which are transitory in nature (strictly speaking, to any effects which last less than $n + 1$ periods), hence there is less reason to worry about the liquidity effect. In addition, by adopting this dependent variable we can more easily examine some interesting aspects of the term-to-maturity structure of interest rates. The use of this variable is a major difference between the tests presented here and those available in the existing literature.

3.4 Test Results

Using the forms of AE and CE derived in (3.26) and (3.27) for autoregressive expectations and consistent expectations, respectively, several regressions of the forms (3.28) and (3.29) were estimated. The real rate of interest was assumed in each case to be constant, or, more generally, orthogonal to the other independent variables. The equation estimated for consistent expectations is of the form

$$r_{t+1} = \rho_{t+1} + \pi^*_{t+1}$$

$$= (\rho + a_1) + \delta_1(L)\pi_{t-1} + \psi_1(L)m_{t-1}. \qquad (3.28)$$

For application, both $\delta_1(L)$ and $\psi_1(L)$ were chosen of order twelve and their coefficients were constrained to satisfy third-order polynomials, with no constraints on the end-points.

The equation estimated for autoregressive expectations is of the form

$$r_{t+1} = \rho_{t+1} + \pi^*_{t+1}$$

$$= (\rho + a_1) + \tau_1(L)\pi_{t-1}. \qquad (3.29)$$

Again $\tau_1(L)$ was chosen to be of order twelve. The coefficients of $\tau_1(L)$ were constrained to satisfy a third-order polynomial, with no constraints on the endpoints.

Operationally, then, we will discriminate between models of consistent and autoregressive expectations based on the significance of $\psi_1(L)$, the distributed lag in money growth rates. Estimates of Equations (3.28) and (3.29), using quarterly data for the United States from 1953:I to 1972:II, are presented in Table 3-1 and Table 3-2. In each regression the dependent variable is the three month interest rate—converted to annual rates—which is expected to prevail from the third to the sixth month in the future. r_{t+1}; this interest rate is computed from basic data on three month Treasury Bill rates and six month Treasury Bill rates.[c]

Our test of the hypothesis of autoregressive expectations against the alternative hypothesis of consistent expectations will be based on the additional

[c]Basic data and sources are presented in the Appendix to this book.

Table 3-1
Parameter Estimates of Equation (3.28),

$$r_{t+1} = (a_1 + \rho) + \delta_1(L)\pi_{t-1} + \psi_1(L)m_{t-1}$$

	$\hat{\delta}(L)$	$\hat{\psi}(L)$	
t-1	.1759 (2.44)	.0905 (2.77)	$(a_1 \hat{+}\rho) = 2.2272$ (9.88)
t-2	.0638 (1.73)	.0683 (4.25)	$\hat{\delta}_1(1) = 0.1213$ (0.87)
t-3	−.0045 (0.12)	.0570 (3.69)	$\hat{\psi}_1(1) = 0.5541$ (5.13)
t-4	−.0374 (0.96)	.0535 (3.06)	
t-5	−.0436 (1.27)	.0550 (3.23)	
t-6	−.0316 (1.18)	.0585 (3.69)	Statistics $R^2 = 0.71$
t-7	−.0101 (0.39)	.0612 (3.74)	$SSE = 39.66$
t-8	.0125 (0.39)	.0600 (3.29)	$N = 65$
t-9	.0275 (0.76)	.0521 (2.71)	$D\text{-}W = 0.98$
t-10	.0264 (0.80)	.0346 (1.90)	
t-11	.0006 (0.02)	.0045 (0.22)	
t-12	−.0584 (0.88)	−.0411 (1.11)	

Notes: Numbers in parentheses below coefficient estimates are absolute values of t ratios, SSE is the sum of squared errors, N is the number of observations, $D-W$ is the Durbin-Watson statistic, both $\delta_1(L)$ and $\psi_1(L)$ are third order polynomials with no endpoint constraints. $\delta_1(1)$ and $\psi_1(1)$ are sums of the coefficient in the respective lag distributions, i.e., L is treated as a dummy variable.

explanatory power yielded by the distributed lag in money growth rates in Equation (3.28). If we find that the coefficients of $\psi_1(L)$ are, when taken as a group, significantly different from zero, then we will be able to reject the hypothesis of AE, as expressed in (3.27) in favor of the hypothesis of CE, as expressed in (3.26). On the other hand, if we find that the group of coefficients in $\psi_1(L)$ are not significantly different from zero then we will be unable to reject AE in favor of CE and will be forced to conclude that the evidence reported is in favor of autoregressive expectations.[d]

[d]This neglects the effects of forecasts of inflation on the real rate of interest discussed by Mundell.[8] According to this view the expectation of inflation results in the substitution of real for monetary capital, driving down the rate of return on real assets.

Table 3-2
Parameter Estimates of Equation (3.29),

	$r_{t+1} = (a_1 + \rho) + \tau_1(L)\pi_{t-1}$	
	$\hat{\tau}_1(L)$	
t-1	.3502	$(a_1 \hat{+} \rho) = 2.6186$
	(4.67)	(9.47)
t-2	.1665	$\hat{\tau}_1(1) = .691641$
	(5.33)	(6.73)
t-3	.0459	
	(1.33)	
t-4	−.0222	Statistics
	(0.55)	$R^2 = 0.49$
t-5	−.0485	
	(1.33)	$SSE = 70.2235$
t-6	−.0436	$N = 65$
	(1.54)	
t-7	−.0182	D-$W = 0.73$
	(0.69)	
t-8	.0171	
	(0.51)	
t-9	.0515	
	(1.35)	
t-10	.0745	
	(2.19)	
t-11	.0753	
	(2.34)	
t-12	.0434	
	(0.60)	

Notes: See Table 3-1. $\tau_1(L)$ satisfies a third-order polynomial with no endpoint constraints.

The test is carried out as follows. I would like to test the hypothesis that $\psi_1(L) = 0$. Table 3-2 presents estimates of (3.29) in which this group of coefficients is constrained to be zero; call the sum of squared residuals from Table 3-2 SSE_2. Table 3-1 presents estimates of (3.28) in which the coefficients of $\psi_1(L)$ are not constrained to zero; call the sum of squared residuals from Table 3-1 SSE_1. To test the hypothesis which interests us we calculate the F-statistic,

$$F = \frac{(SEE_2 - SEE_1)/m}{SEE_1/(n-k)} , \tag{3.30}$$

where n is the number of observations, k is the number of independent parameters in Equation (3.28), and m is the number of constraints imposed on these parameters by Equation (3.29). In this model $n = 65$, $k = 9$, and $m = 4$.

Thus we obtain an F-statistic valued at

$$F(4,56) = 10.71, \tag{3.31}$$

which is seen to be highly significant—the critical F-value is around 2.5 for a .05 level of significance and around 3.7 for a .01 level of significance—and are able to reject the hypothesis of autoregressive expectations as represented by (3.29), in favor of the alternative hypothesis of consistent expectations, as represented by (3.28).

The low Durbin-Watson statistics of Tables 3-1 and 3-2 indicate the presence of positive serial correlation. This tends to bias the test toward rejecting hypotheses that state that some of the coefficients are zero. I have adjusted for serial correlation by estimating each equation using the Cochrane-Orcutt technique, which yields an approximation to generalized least squares. Operationally, the procedure adds $\hat{\lambda}$ (lagged residual) to the r.h.s. of the equation, where $\hat{\lambda}$ is an estimate of the first-order serial correlation coefficient; an iterative technique is employed to find the value of $\hat{\lambda}$ which minimizes the standard error of the estimate. For Equation (3.28) the Cochrane-Orcutt procedure resulted in $SSE = 27.7375$, for a final value of $\hat{\lambda} = .589$; for Equation (3.29) the result is $SSE = 37.8902$, for a final value of $\hat{\lambda} = .724$. The F-statistic for the hypothesis that $\psi_1(L) = 0$ is, in this case, of value $F = 5.04$. We are again forced to reject the hypothesis of AE in favor of the alternative hypothesis of CE.

As a further check on the results I have reestimated Equations (3.28) and (3.29) using geometric lag distributions, rather than the polynomial constraints used in the estimates presented in Tables 3-1 and 3-2. The results were remarkably similar; the F-statistic corresponding to (3.30) is $F = 10.12$. The mean lag of money growth rates behind expected rates of inflation is again about five to seven quarters.

Since I am using a rather novel dependent variable, it may be suggested that the results in favor of CE are due to the particular specification of the variable used. This is not the case; the hypothesis of autoregressive expectations must be rejected in all of a wide variety of models using alternative spot rates of interest as dependent variables. The F-statistics corresponding to (3.30) are; $F = 29.08$ for the three month Treasury Bill rate; $F = 22.93$ for the six month Treasury Bill rate; $F = 26.04$ for the rate on four to six month Prime Commercial Paper; and $F = 20.85$ for the rate on AAA Corporate Bonds. The patterns of the coefficients of the lag distributions and the estimates of their means are all quite similar to those reported in Tables 3-1 and 3-2.

3.5 Evidence Concerning A Corollary Hypothesis

I believe that there is widespread agreement in the economics profession that the lags in forming expectations are very long, a belief that I have argued, in Chapter

2, is due to a false view of the estimates presented by Irving Fisher. Relevant quotes from Sargent and Friedman are:

. . . Those studies have usually invoked the hypothesis that the public's anticipated rate of inflation is given by a distributed lag in the actual rate of inflation. Combining this specification with Fisher's formula has led to regressing the nominal rate of interest against current and past rates of inflation. With a few exceptions, the result of this procedure has been to produce estimates of extraordinarily long distributed lags, lags that have been imputed to a tendency of the public to form its expectations of inflation with a very long lag.[9]

. . . and let the public come to expect that prices will continue to rise. Borrowers will then be willing to pay and lenders will demand higher interest rates . . . as Irving Fisher pointed out decades ago. This price expectation effect is slow to develop and slow to disappear.[10]

From the estimates presented in Tables 3-1 and 3-2 we can get information about the length of this lag. The mean of $\psi_1(L)$, the lag distribution between money growth rates and expected inflation, is estimated to be 3.54 quarters. Remember, however, that we are measuring the expected rate of inflation in period $t + 1$ and we are exclusively using information on money growth rates prior to period $t - 1$. The mean of the lag distribution between money growth rates and the expected rate of inflation, then, is approximately 5.54 quarters, or about a year and a half. This is not far from the mean of the lag which we would expect to find between money growth rates and actual rates of inflation in the United States over the same period. Examination of our estimate of $\delta_1(L)$, the lag distribution between past actual inflation and expected inflation reveals that the weights fall off quite rapidly, implying the absence of a long lag. The evidence presented here is not consistent with a "molasses world" where people stubbornly refuse to alter their forecasts when presented with new information. It is, rather, consistent with a world in which rational individuals gather information about the process which generates inflation.

3.6 Further Extentions and Conclusions

This chapter presented a model of investor behavior with special reference to the choice of the amount and mix of alternative sources of information available in the market. It then presented a hypothesis of the way in which market participants forecast inflation and tested this hypothesis against the leading alternative in the literature, autoregressive expectations. I found that over the period since 1953, autoregressive expectations is much inferior to the hypothesis developed in Section 3.2, consistent expectations. This is evidence that the tacit assumption in all autoregressive models of expectations—that other types of information are too costly relative to their return to be collected by investors—is not justified by experience in the United States over the sample period. This result also suggests that tests of hypotheses which have been carried out in such models should be viewed with caution, until they have also been tested under more general assumptions about the formation of expectations.

It is also likely that our tests have also been guilty of specification errors, but of a more modest magnitude than those committed by users of *AE*. There are likely other sources of information which are exploited by investors in forecasting inflation, since there are others which economists see fit to include in their macromodels. Further work on testing and specifying alternative, more general, models of forecast formation is warranted.

In the next chapter we will examine in more detail the precise relationship between the theories of the economist and the forecasts of the investor, in the context of rational expectations.

4 Rational Expectations of Inflation

The hypothesis of Consistent Expectations has been advanced and tested in earlier chapters. We saw that individuals will, in general, find it to their own advantage to form predictions about the future behavior of the rate of inflation, since the rate of inflation is, at a point in time, the rate at which one's holdings of assets fixed in nominal terms is shrinking in real value. We view forecasting, in the model presented in Chapter 3, as a productive activity. The inputs are time and labor along with different amounts of information which the producer has collected. The amount of each type of information collected depends ˜on the costs of collection and assimilation of the information and on the value of the additional units, and on the transactions costs which inhibit joint production of forecasts. Each source of information will be exploited until the marginal cost of exploiting a source equals the marginal return from doing so. Thus we assume that somehow individual traders have more or less accurate ideas of which types of information it is profitable to collect and use, i.e., they have in their minds the information contained in a forecast production function. In this chapter we will assume that once they have information about the production function, other costs of collecting and using information are essentially zero. This implies that they will be exploited until further units are worthless, i.e., so that $d(f[S])/dS = 0$. Likewise we will assume that the costs and rewards are such that economists have acquired all valuable information in increasing the accuracy of *their* forecasts of inflation. In fact, one of the insights of the "rational expectations" hypothesis is that economists and investors gather information for the same reasons, and under the same analytical framework.

Earlier we maintained that those who trade in the market gain insights into the workings of the economy by observing certain time-ordered relationships among economic magnitudes. In this way they assimilate information about the structure of the economy. For instance, they might recognize that in certain situations the time series of inflation rates exhibits substantial first-order serial correlation, or that wars are generally accompanied by high rates of inflation regardless of the behavior of the price level over the preceding periods, or that high and sustained rates of growth of the money stock lead to high rates of inflation. These are the types of conditional statements about the actual behavior of the economy which the trader brings together to form a forecast production function.

Economists, like investors, produce forecasts of economic magnitudes. The inputs into their forecasts are qualitatively the same; time, labor, and alternative types of information in varying amounts. The forecasts of inflation made by an economist will also depend upon his view of the structure of the economy. The production function for forecasting, showing the alternative combinations of information which can be used to forecast with varying precision, is analogous to the economist's collection of theories. Under certain assumptions about the costs of collecting information, the relevant theory of the economist should closely approximate the actual structure of the economy, and the predictions of the economist should resemble those which would be made from a "true" reduced form of the economy.

But what of the predictions made by the market trader? They should also approximate those which would be made if one knew the true structure of the economy; the degree of approximation would be closer, the cheaper the information to collect and process. The idea that market participants have incentives to gather information about the structure of the economy and thus that the forecasts of investors depend upon the structure of the economy, was forcefully advanced by John F. Muth;

... I should like to suggest that expectations, since they are informed predictions of future events, are *essentially the same as the predictions of the relevant economic theory* ... we call such expectations 'rational' ... the hypothesis can be rephrased a little more precisely as follows: that expectations of firms (or, more generally, the subjective probability distributions of outcomes) tend to be distributed, for the same information set, about the predictions of the theory (or the 'objective' probability distributions of outcomes).[1]

The plausibility of rational expectations is apparent. It is common in economics to assume rationality in almost every other activity; consistent treatment requires that we view the purchase and use of information like that of any other commodity, as a basic object of choice to the consumer, in the manner presented in Section 3.1.

4.1 Rational Expectations and Autoregressive Models

Unfortunately, the concept of rational expectations has remained largely unexploited in the literature. The models presented by Muth[2] to illustrate the hypothesis of rational expectations were market equilibrium models with a *single* exogenous (stochastic) process. The result of this feature was that the rational expectation which would be formed by traders in full knowledge of the structure of the market was reducible to autoregressive form; the rational expectation of future market price in such a market is a weighted sum of past realized prices. Since the only information needed to produce optimal forecasts in this market is past price behavior, it is difficult to see how knowledge of the structure pays off to the forecaster.

Had Muth chosen to include another exogenous process in his models, the rational expectation of market price would no longer be expressible in auto-regressive form, but would in the general case be reducible to a mixed autoregressive moving-average representation.[a] Nelson concludes that,

... it is perhaps because of this obscuring of the full implications of the theory that the term 'rational expectations' has degenerated in current usage to little more than a synonym for unbiased or for the absence of patently suboptimal properties such as serial correlation in prediction errors.[3]

We can illustrate the above result by examining the rational expectation of inflation in two alternative models. The analysis that follows is an adaptation of arguments presented by Nelson.[4] I have altered Nelson's notation and framed the analysis in terms of the rational expectation of inflation, rather than Nelson's more general result. The result, nevertheless, that "rational expectations are not general extrapolative" is entirely Nelson's.

Let π_t be the rate of inflation in period t. We will view π_t as an endogenous variable in a system determined by N exogenous processes ($X_1, \ldots X_N$). We wish to show that, when $N = 1$, the rational expectation of inflation π_t^* for period t formed on the basis of information available in period $t - 1$ *can* be expressed extrapolatively; and that when $N = 2$ or larger this is *no longer true,* i.e., the rational expectation of inflation, π_t^*, *cannot* be expressed extrapolatively.

Case 1: N = 1

Let π_t be represented by the reduced form in $X_1 = X$:

$$\pi_t = \theta X_t + a_0 \tag{4.1}$$

where θ is some combination of the parameters of the structural system and a_0 is a constant. Also, let $\{X_t\}$ be a linear stochastic process which is driven by the white noise process $\{u_t\}$, i.e., $\{u_t\}$ is a zero mean, constant variance, serially uncorrelated stochastic process. We have that:

$$X_t = u_t + \phi_1 u_{t-1} + \ldots + \phi_q u_{t-q}$$

$$= (1 + \phi_1 L + \ldots + \phi_q L^q) u_t = \phi(L) u_t \tag{4.2}$$

---

[a]Nelson shows that in the general case where the rational expectation of a variable is represented by the sum of two or more stationary stochastic processes, it is not possible to reduce the rational expectation to a simple extrapolation of the past history of the variable being forecast. I wish to thank Nelson for permission to quote this penetrating study, and for helpful discussion of these results.

Given (4.1) this implies that the current value of the endogenous variable can be expressed as:

$$\pi_t = \theta\phi(L)u_t + a_0. \tag{4.3}$$

If the roots of $\phi(L)$ all lie outside the unit circle[b] then $\phi(L)$ possesses an inverse and we can write,

$$\phi^{-1}(L)\pi_t = \theta u_t + a_1,$$

where the coefficients of $\phi^{-1}(L)$ can be found by matching coefficients of L^i in the relation of $\phi^{-1}(L)\phi(L) = 1$. This expresses π_t as a mixed autoregressive moving-average process. Equivalently, we have

$$\pi_t = \psi(L)\pi_{t-1} + \theta u_t + a_1, \tag{4.4}$$

where $\psi(L)$ is such that $\phi^{-1}(L) = 1 - \psi(L)L$. The rational expectation of inflation π_t^* is that which would be formed by traders in full knowledge of the structure of the process generating inflation, and of the stochastic properties of the exogenous process, and is formed by taking the expected value of (4.4).

$$\pi_t^* = \psi(L)\pi_{t-1} + \theta E(u_t) + a_1 = \psi(L)\pi_{t-1} + a_1. \tag{4.5}$$

The latter can be recognized as an autoregressive forecast based on past realized values of the rate of inflation.

Case 2: N = 2

Let π_t be represented by the reduced-form of a system with two exogenous variables X and Y,

$$\pi_t = \theta X_t + \gamma Y_t + a_0. \tag{4.6}$$

where, again Θ and γ are combinations of the parameters of the structural model, a_0 is a constant, and $\{X_t\}$ and $\{Y_t\}$ are discrete linear stochastic processes driven, respectively, by the white noise processes $\{u_t\}$ and $\{v_t\}$;

$$X_t = u_t + \phi_1 u_{t-1} + \ldots + \phi_q u_{t-q}$$

$$= (1 + \phi_1 L + \ldots + \phi_q L^q)u_t = \phi(L)u_t; \tag{4.7}$$

---

[b]See Chapter 3, footnote b, for discussion of this condition for invertibility.

$$Y_t = v_t + \xi_1 v_{t-1} + \ldots + \xi_p v_{t-p}$$

$$= (1 + \xi_1 L + \ldots + \xi_p L^p) v_t = \xi(L) v_t. \tag{4.8}$$

These together with (4.6) imply that we can express the endogenous variable as:

$$\pi_t = \theta \phi(L) u_t + \gamma \xi(L) v_t + a_0. \tag{4.9}$$

Given that all the roots of $\phi(L)$ lie outside the unit circle it has an inverse and we can write:

$$\phi^{-1}(L)\pi_t = \theta u_t + \gamma \phi^{-1}(L)\xi(L)v_t + a_1 \tag{4.10}$$

expressing the rate of inflation as a mixed autoregressive moving average process, hence that:

$$\pi_t = \delta(L)\pi_{t-1} + \gamma \phi^{-1}(L)\xi(L)v_t + \theta u_t + a_1, \tag{4.11}$$

To facilitate taking the expectation π_t^* of (4.11) let us separate the second term of (4.11) into the stochastic component and the deterministic component and define

$$\phi^{-1}(L)v_t = v_t + \phi^{-1}(L)'\xi(L)'v_{t-1} \tag{4.12}$$

so that (4.11) can be written as

$$\pi_t = \delta(L)\pi_{t-1} + \gamma v_t + \gamma \phi^{-1}(L)'\xi(L)'v_{t-1} + \theta u_t + a_1. \tag{4.13}$$

The rational expectation of inflation π_t^* is defined by taking the expectation of (4.13):

$$\pi_t^* = \delta(L)\pi_{t-1} + \gamma \phi^{-1}(L)'\xi(L)'v_{t-1} + a_1. \tag{4.14}$$

This is the expected value of inflation made by a forecaster with complete knowledge of the process which generates inflation of the stochastic properties of the exogenous inputs, and of the past histories of all variables up to and including period $t-1$. This expectation cannot be expressed as a weighted sum of previous values of inflation; it must in general use information from $n-1$ of the exogenous variables plus the past history of inflation, or, alternatively, from all n of the exogenous processes. Furthermore, rational expectations must, in general, be more efficient than extrapolations (in the sense of smaller mean square error) because a larger information set is used in forecasting.[5]

This analysis does not imply that real-world forecasts of market traders will be formed with full knowledge of the structure and of *all* of the exogenous processes. Costs of gathering information might, following the analysis presented in Chapter 3, imply that it is only worthwhile to gather information on a small fraction of the exogenous variables which enter the reduced form equation for inflation. It *does* imply that investors may find it worthwhile to learn about the structure of the economy and to exploit that knowledge in forecasting, and that there will be some correspondence between the theories of the economist and the forecasts of the market trader. More importantly, it casts serious doubt on the efficacy of autoregressive expectations models, including extrapolative, adaptive, and error-learning expectations mechanisms, when those expectations are presumed to be rational.[c]

The aim of the empirical work presented in this chapter is to test the rationality of market expectations of inflation, as revealed in certain market rates of interest, in the more restrictive sense of Muth, discussed above. To do this it will not suffice to examine expectations data to see whether or not the same types of information are used as those which appear in the reduced form equation of the economist, as we did in Chapter 3. We must also test whether or not these types of information are used *in the same way* in both sets of data. We will do this under two alternative assumptions about the determination of the real rate of interest.

4.2 A Simple Model of Inflation

Before we can test the hypothesis that expectations of inflation are formed rationally we must specify the exogenous variables which are likely to appear as arguments in the reduced form equation for inflation implicit in the structure of the economy.,

$$\pi_t = f(X_1, \ldots, X_n). \tag{4.15}$$

I will adopt a simple model of the macroeconomy given by eight equations.[d]

$c = f(y,r)$	(4.16a)		$M^d = Ph(y,r)$	(4.16e)	
$I = g(r)$	(4.16b)		$M^s = M_0$	(4.16f)	
$G = G_0$	(4.16c)		$M^d = M^s$	(4.16g)	(4.16)
$y = c + I + G/P$	(4.16d)		$y = y_0 e^{\lambda t}$	(4.16h)	

[c]Nelson summarizes, "It is the fact that rational expectations are not general extrapolative which suggests how knowledge of economic structure pays off in predictive efficiency, namely, economic agents are able to utilize appropriately a larger information set."[6] "This implies that serious errors of specification may arise if expectations are actually formed rationally, but in an empirical model they are regarded as functions of past history alone. . . ."[7]

[d]This model is almost identical to the "Simple Common Model"[8] of Friedman. Several points, however, have been taken from McCallum's variant[9] of this model.

c	= real consumption	r	= interest rate
y	= real income	P	= price level
I	= real investment	M^d	= money demanded
G	= nominal government spending	M^s	= money supplied
		t	= time

The first four equations describe the adjustment of savings and investment flows; the next three describe the adjustment of money demanded and supplied. The last equation states that output is always at full-employment, and that full-employment output grows exponentially at the rate λ over time.

If we were to exclude (4.16h), the remaining equations would form a model which Friedman maintains "would be accepted alike by adherents of the quantity theory and of the income-expenditure theory."[10] Note, however, that Equations (4.16a) through (4.16g) do not form a closed system; there are eight variables: $c, y, r, I, G, M^d, P, M^s$, but only seven equations.

I have chosen to complete the system by adding (4.16h) which requires the level of output to be fixed at full-employment at a given time, and further specifies that full-employment output grows exponentially over time at the rate λ. The justification for this assumption concerns the relative speeds of two alternative adjustments implicit in our model.

Let us examine the system (4.16) as it progresses through time in response to changing exogenous variables. These exogenous shocks can be viewed as having two separate effects. The immediate effect is to disturb the system from its equilibrium value implied by (4.16). For example, a change in the money supply will cause a temporary deviation of real output from its equilibrium value (full employment). In addition there will be a new set of equilibrium values for the endogenous variables in the system. For example, a change in the money supply will imply a new equilibrium price level, which will be realized once prices have fully adjusted.

The aim of this Section is to analyze the dynamic adjustment of equilibrium prices to exogenous disturbances. Our concern here is proper treatment of the other dynamic process in our model, that of adjustment of actual output to equilibrium output.

Professor Samuelson, in a discussion of dynamic adjustment paths remarks,

I, myself, find it convenient to visualize equilibrium processes of quite different speed, some very slow compared to others. Within each long run there is a shorter run, and within each shorter run there is a still shorter run, and so forth in an infinite regression. For analytic purposes it is often convenient to treat slow processes as data and concentrate upon the processes of interest. . . .

So to speak we are able, by *ceteris paribus* assumptions to disregard the changes in variables subject to motions much "slower" than the ones under consideration; . . . At the same time *we are able to abstract from the behavior of processes much "faster" than the ones under consideration,* . . . *by the assumption that they* are rapidly damped and *can be supposed to have worked out their effects.* . . . If one can be sure that the system is stable and strongly damped, there is no great harm in neglecting to analyze the exact path from one equilibrium to another, and in taking refuge in the *mutatis mutandis* assumption.[11]

We are concerned with the determination of dynamic adjustments of the price level in response to changing exogenous variables. We assume that the dynamic adjustment of real output to its equilibrium level is very rapid relative to adjustments in the equilibrium price level over time. Thus we greatly simplify our analysis by assuming that real output adjusts instantaneously to full-employment output. Thus we can concentrate on changes in equilibrium values of the system (4.16) and avoid detailed analysis of macroeconomic disequilibrium.

Thus our *mutatis mutandis* assumption of full-employment income adds to this system (4.16) the Walrasian equations of general equilibrium, as a higher-order block in a block recursive system containing (4.16). This assumption is appropriate only for the study of changes in the price level and only if our assumption about relative adjustment speeds is true.

The endogenous variables in (4.16) are y, r, P, M^d: the exogenous variables are M, G, and t. Assume that f, g, and h are continuously differentiable functions and that $0 < f_y < 1, f_r > 0, g' < 0, h_y > 0$, and $h_r < 0$. We can then solve for the endogenous variables in (4.16) in terms of the values of the exogenous variables.

$$P = f_1(M,G,t) \quad (4.17a) \qquad r = f_3(M,G,t) \quad (4.17c)$$
$$y = f_2(M,G,t) \quad (4.17b) \qquad M^d = f_4(M,G,t) \quad (4.17d) \quad (4.17)$$

The reduced form equation in (4.17) of special interest in this study is (4.17a), the equation determining the equilibrium price level in terms of the stock of money, the rate of government spending, and time. I shall assume a discrete log-linear specification of (4.17a),

$$\log P_t = \alpha_0 + \alpha_1 \log M_t + \alpha_1 \log G_t + \alpha_3 t, \qquad (4.18)$$

operate on (4.18) by $(1 - L)$ to get

$$\Delta \log P_t = \alpha_1 \Delta \log M_t + \alpha_2 \Delta \log G_t + \alpha_3, \qquad (4.19)$$

or approximately, in the notation of Chapter 3,

$$\pi_t = a_0 + \theta m_t + \gamma v_t. \qquad (4.20)$$

A common assumption at this point is to introduce a partial adjustment mechanism into (4.20) by inserting π_{t-1} into the r.h.s. of (4.20) with a positive coefficient. This is equivalent to assuming an identical distributed lag on each of the right-hand-side variables in (4.20). I opt for the less restrictive, but formally similar, assumption that each of the variables in (4.20) affects the rate of inflation with a distributed lag, but one which may be unique to the particular variable. Thus we have

$$\pi_t = a_0 + \theta \phi (L) m_t + \gamma \xi (L) v_t, \tag{4.21}$$

where, of course, v_t is the percent change in government spending in period t, and m_t is the percent rate of change in the stock of money in period t, and $\phi(L)$ and $\xi(L)$ are polynomials in the lag operator.

Now (4.21) can be treated as an example of the model (4.9) which involves interpreting both $\{m_t\}$ and $\{v_t\}$ as white noise processes. Actually, for analytical rigor, $\{m_t - \overline{m}_t\}$ would more closely approximate a white noise process, where $\overline{m}_t$ is the mean value of money growth over some previous period; using the simple growth rate in (4.21), however, merely involves a reinterpretation of the constant term. This specification of the model implies that the weights of $\phi(L)$ are the interim multipliers for the rate of money growth; similarly the weights of $\xi(L)$ are interpreted as the interim multipliers of the rate of change of government spending. If we treat the lag operator as a dummy variable, then $\phi(1)$ refers to the total effect on the rate of inflation of a sustained unit rise in the rate of money growth, and $\xi(1)$ is a measure of the total effect on the rate of inflation of a unit increase in the rate of change of the level of government spending.

4.3 Rational Forecasts

We can now develop representations for rational forecasts. Assume that all latent roots of $\xi(L)$ lie outside the unit circle, so that it has an inverse, and write

$$\xi^{-1}(L)\pi_t = \theta \xi^{-1}(L)\phi(L)m_t + \gamma v_t + \xi^{-1}(L)a_0, \tag{4.22}$$

which implies that

$$\pi_t = a_1 + \theta \xi^{-1}(L)\phi(L)m_t + \gamma v_t + \delta(L)\pi_{t-1}. \tag{4.23}$$

To form the rational forecast of the rate of inflation[e] in period t, π_t^*, made on the basis of information available in period $(t-1)$ is,

$$\pi_t^* = \theta \xi^{-1}(L)'\phi(L)'m_{t-1} + \delta(L)\pi_{t-1} + a_1, \tag{4.24}$$

---

[e]Lucas, in an imaginative paper,[12] applies the hypothesis of rational expectations to the accelerationist controversy. Lucas develops rational expectations from reduced form relations, similar to our analysis below.

where the primed polynomials indicate the absence of the coefficient attached to current money growth (the properties of the white noise processes dictate that $E(m_t) = E(v_t) = 0$). A test of the rationality of forecasts of inflation can now be performed in two steps. The first is to estimate equations like (4.24) where the observed rate of inflation serves as the dependent variable. This will indicate the way in which rational forecasts would be formed. The second is to estimate relationships between the expected rate of inflation and these same variables, and check whether or not the information is used in the same way as in the reduced-form of the structure generating inflation.

State this more explicitly by noting that the rational forecast of inflation, π_t^*, would be formed according to

$$\pi_t^* = \psi(L)m_{t-1} + \delta(L)\pi_{t-1} + a_1, \tag{4.25}$$

where, to simplify notation, I have written $\psi(L) = \theta\xi^{-1}(L)'\phi(L)'$ and made the substitution in (4.24).

Now operate on (4.25) by F, the forward-shift operator, to obtain,

$$\pi_{t+1}^* = \psi(L)m_t + \delta(L)\pi_t + a_1. \tag{4.26}$$

Apply Wold's "chain principle of forecasting," as in Chapter 3, by replacing the stochastic elements on the r.h.s. of (4.26) with their expected values,

$$\pi_{t+1}^* = \psi(L)'m_{t-1} + \delta_0\pi_t^* + (\delta_1 + \delta_2 L + \ldots)\pi_{t-1} + a_1. \tag{4.27}$$

Now replace π_t^* of (4.27) with the equivalent r.h.s. of (4.24) to obtain,

$$\pi_{t+1}^* = \psi_1(L)m_{t-1} + \delta_1(L)\pi_{t-1} + a_1, \tag{4.28}$$

where $\psi_1(L)$ and $\delta_1(L)$ are new lag polynomials. $\psi_1(L)$ is derived from $\psi(L)$ by deleting ψ_0, operating on the resulting polynomial by the forward-shift operator, F, and adding $\delta_0\psi(L)$. The relationship between the coefficients of $\delta_1(L)$ and $\delta(L)$ was shown in the text immediately following Equation (3.26) of Chapter 3.

An investor would form a rational expectation of π_{t+1} on the basis of information available in period $(t-1)$ by gathering information on the parameters of the forecasting Equation (4.28), i.e., by regressing actual π_{t+1} on distributed lags of money growth and realized inflation and a constant term,

$$\pi_{t+1} = a_1 + \psi_1(L)m_{t-1} + \delta_1(L)\pi_{t-1}. \tag{4.29}$$

Table 4-1 presents estimates of (4.29) for the United States, over the period from 1953:I to 1972:II, using quarterly data. Both $\psi_1(L)$ and $\delta_1(L)$ are constrained to satisfy third-order polynomials with no endpoint constraints.

Table 4-1
Parameter Estimates of Equation (4.29),

$$\pi_{t+1} = a_1 + \psi_1(L)m_{t-1} + \delta_1(L)\pi_{t-1}$$

	$\hat{\psi}_1(L)$	$\hat{\delta}_1(L)$	
t-1	0.281	−.0410	$\hat{a}_1 = .5082$
	(0.47)	(0.32)	(1.26)
t-2	.0747	.0793	$\hat{\psi}_1(1) = .7274$
	(2.58)	(1.19)	(3.79)
t-3	.0982	.1290	$\hat{\delta}_1(1) = -.0764$
	(3.52)	(2.05)	(0.30)
t-4	.1035	.1244	
	(3.27)	(1.87)	
t-5	.0954	.0815	Statistics
	(3.09)	(1.39)	
t-6	.0787	.0166	$R^2 = 0.49$
	(2.74)	(0.35)	$SSE = 129.453$
t-7	.0583	−.0542	$N = 65$
	(1.98)	(1.17)	$D\text{-}W = 1.84$
t-8	.0389	−.1149	
	(1.18)	(2.00)	
t-9	.0254	−.1492	
	(0.73)	(2.32)	
t-10	.0226	−.1410	
	(0.69)	(2.41)	
t-11	.0353	−.0742	
	(0.97)	(1.30)	
t-12	.0684	.0674	
	(1.02)	(0.56)	

Notes: See notes to Table 3-1, Chapter 3. $\psi_1(L)$ and $\delta_1(L)$ satisfy third-order polynomials with no endpoint restrictions.

Now I will estimate the way in which investors actually incorporate information contained in past rates of money growth and past rates of inflation into forecasts. We would like to accomplish this by estimating,

$$\pi^*_{t+1} = a'_1 + \psi'_1(L)m_{t-1} + \delta'_1(L)\pi_{t-1}, \tag{4.30}$$

where the primed polynomials indicate that the lag polynomials in (4.30) may be different than the corresponding polynomials in (4.29).

Since, however, we have no direct observations on forecasts of inflation we shall proceed by recognizing, as in Chapter 3, that in equilibrium the market rate of interest must approximately equal the real rate of interest plus the expected rate of inflation, all defined over the same time period;

$$r_t = \rho_t + \pi^*_t. \tag{4.31}$$

Clearly this must also hold for forward, or expected, rates of interest as well; operate on (4.31) by F to obtain

$$r_{t+1} = \rho_{t+1} + \pi^*_{t+1},\qquad(4.32)$$

where r_{t+1} is the one-period expected rate of interest, for period ($t + 1$), based on information available in period ($t - 1$). If we assume, as we did earlier, that the real rate of interest is constant, then we can substitute (4.30) into (4.32) to get,

$$r_{t+1} = a'_1 + \rho + \psi'_1(L)m_{t-1} + \delta'_1(L)\pi_{t-1}.\qquad(4.33)$$

Table 4-2 presents estimates of (4.33) reproduced from Chapter 3. The dependent variable, r_{t+1} is computed from yields on three month and six month Treasury Bills, as in (3.22) of Chapter 3.

Table 4-2
Parameter Estimates of Equation (4.33),

$$r_{t+1} = (a'_1 + \rho) + \psi'_1(L)m_{t-1} + \delta'_1(L)\pi_{t-1}$$

	$\hat{\psi}'_1(L)$	$\hat{\delta}'_1(L)$	
t-1	.0905 (2.77)	.1759 (2.44)	$(a'_1 + \rho) = 2.2272$ (9.88)
t-2	.0683 (4.25)	.0638 (1.73)	$\hat{\psi}'_1(1) = 0.5541$ (5.13)
t-3	.0570 (3.69)	−.0045 (0.12)	$\hat{\delta}'_1(1) = 0.1213$ (0.87)
t-4	.0535 (3.06)	−.0374 (0.96)	
t-5	.0550 (3.23)	−.0436 (1.27)	Statistics
t-6	.0585 (3.69)	−.0316 (1.18)	$R^2 = 0.71$ $SSE = 39.66$
t-7	.0612 (3.74)	−.0101 (0.39)	$N = 65$
t-8	−.0600 (3.29)	.0125 (0.39)	$D\text{-}W = 0.98$
t-9	.0521 (2.71)	.0275 (0.76)	
t-10	.0346 (1.90)	.0264 (0.80)	
t-11	.0045 (0.22)	.0006 (0.02)	
t-12	−.0411 (1.11)	−.0584 (0.88)	

Notes: See notes to Table 3-1, Chapter 3. $\psi'_1(L)$ and $\delta'_1(L)$ satisfy third-order polynomials with no endpoint restrictions.

To test whether or not forecasts of inflation were formed rationally during our sample we test the hypothesis that,

$$H_0 : \begin{bmatrix} \psi_1'(L) \\ \\ \delta_1'(L) \end{bmatrix} = \begin{bmatrix} \psi_1(L) \\ \\ \delta_1(L) \end{bmatrix} \tag{4.34}$$

against the alternative hypothesis that they are not equal. Operationally, this is accomplished by subtracting Equation (4.29) from Equation (4.33). The result is,

$$r_{t+1} - \pi_{t+1} = (a_1' + \rho - a_1) + [\psi_1'(L) - \psi_1(L)] m_{t-1}$$
$$+ [\delta_1'(L) - \delta_1(L)] \pi_{t-1}. \tag{4.35}$$

If the hypothesis of rational expectations, as set out in (4.34), is true, then we would expect the distributed lags in past rates of inflation and money growth in Equation (4.35) to have virtually no explanatory power. If the value of the F-statistic for the regression as a whole, then, exceeds a suitably chosen critical value we will be forced to reject the hypothesis of rational forecasting in this model. Table 4-3 presents the result of estimating (4.35) for the United States over the period 1953:I to 1972:II with quarterly data. The constraints imposed on the coefficients of the lag polynomials were chosen to agree with those of Tables 4-1 and 4-2, i.e., third-order with no endpoint restrictions. This implies that there are eight scrambled parameters plus the constant term to be estimated in (4.35); we have sixty-five observations. Hence the proper F-statistic is $F_{.05}(8,56)$ for a .05 level of significance, which is about 2.1. The value of the F-statistic for the equation presented in Table 4-3, $F = 1.01$, suggests that we are unable to reject the hypothesis of rational expectations in this model; the evidence is consistent with that hypothesis.

As a check on these results I have conducted the test using an alternative dependent variable that does not require the validity of the expectations hypothesis of the term structure of interest rates, nor of the chain principle of forecasting.

An investor would form the rational expectation π_t^* by noting (4.25), then estimating the parameters of $\psi(L)$ and of $\delta(L)$ by estimating the regression equation,

$$\pi_t = a_1 + \psi(L)m_{t-1} + \delta(L)\pi_{t-1}. \tag{4.36}$$

Suppose that expectations are actually formed according to,

$$\pi_t^* = a_1' + \psi'(L)m_{t-1} + \delta'(L)\pi_{t-1}, \tag{4.37}$$

Table 4-3
Parameter Estimates of Equation (4.35),

$$r_{t+1} - \pi_{t+1} = (a_1' + \rho - a_1) + [\psi_1'(L) - \psi_1(L)]m_{t-1} + [\delta_1'(L) - \delta(L)]\pi_{t-1}$$

	$[\psi_1'(L) \hat{-} \psi_1(L)]$	$[\delta_1'(L) \hat{-} \delta(L)]$		
t-1	.0615	.1938	$(a_1' + \hat{\rho} - a_1)$	= 1.6247
	(0.93)	(1.35)		(3.62)
t-2	−.0052	−.0131	$[\psi_1'(1) \hat{-} \psi_1(1)]$ =	.1832
	(0.16)	(0.18)		(0.84)
t-3	−.0391	−.1174	$[\delta_1'(1) \hat{-} \delta(1)]$ =	.2479
	(1.26)	(1.67)		(0.88)
t-4	−.0479	−.1414		
	(1.36)	(1.91)		
t-5	−.0390	−.1071	Statistics	
	(1.13)	(1.64)	R^2 =	0.13
t-6	−.0199	−.0369	SSE =	160.492
	(0.62)	(0.71)	N =	65
t-7	.0019	.0471	D-W =	1.89
	(0.06)	(0.91)		
t-8	.0189	.1226		
	(0.52)	(1.92)		
t-9	.0235	.1675		
	(0.61)	(2.34)		
t-10	.0083	.1596		
	(0.23)	(2.45)		
t-11	−.0343	.0766		
	(0.84)	(1.20)		
t-12	−.1118	−.1036		
	(1.50)	(0.78)		

Notes: See notes to Table 3-1, Chapter 3. $[\psi_1'(L) - \psi_1(L)]$ and $[\delta_1'(L) - \delta(L)]$ satisfy third-order polynomials with no endpoint restrictions.

where, again, the primes indicate that the lag polynomials may be different than their counterparts in Equation (4.36).

Combine (4.31) and (4.36) to get,

$$r_t = a_1' + \rho + \psi'(L)m_{t-1} + \delta'(L)\pi_{t-1}. \tag{4.38}$$

Now we subtract (4.36) from (4.38) to get

$$r_t - \pi_t = (a_1' + \rho - a_1) + (\psi'(L) - \psi(L))m_{t-1} + (\delta'(L) - \delta(L))\pi_{t-1} \tag{4.39}$$

which is similar in form to (4.35), with an important exception; the interest rate on the left hand side of (4.39) is a "spot," or market, rate of interest, which is observable in the market.

The hypothesis of rational expectations, in this model, again reduces to a test of the equality of the coefficients of the corresponding lag polynomials,

$$
H_0: \quad \begin{bmatrix} \psi'(L) \\ \delta'(L) \end{bmatrix} = \begin{bmatrix} \psi(L) \\ \delta(L) \end{bmatrix} \tag{4.40}
$$

Estimating (4.39), and testing the significance of the regression will serve as a test of the hypothesis of rational expectations. The F-statistic for the regression Equation (4.39) is $F = 1.97$, using the three month Treasury Bill rate, which leads us to conclude that the evidence is consistent with the hypothesis of rational expectations when using a *spot* rate of interest.

A possible criticism of these results, and of those presented in Table 4-3, is that each of the polynomials $\psi'(L)$, $\psi(L)$, $\delta'(L)$, and $\delta(L)$ is zero, hence the hypothesis (4.40) is satisfied for reasons other than rational expectations. A brief glance at the evidence presented in this chapter, however, will disqualify this criticism. The F-statistics for the regression equations corresponding to Tables 4-1 and 4-2 for the three month Treasury Bill rate are, respectively, $F = 6.63$ and $F = 32.64$.

4.4 The Crude Quantity Theory and Rational Expectations

It is of some interest to examine an even simpler model of the determination of the rate of inflation which is suggested by the crude quantity theory of money. Let the money supply be exogenously determined and velocity be regarded as constant then

$$
M = kPy \tag{4.41}
$$

can be transformed into

$$
\Delta \log P = \Delta \log M - \Delta \log y, \tag{4.42}
$$

and if we make the assumption that y is always at its full employment level, and that capacity output grows at a constant rate, then (4.42) becomes

$$
\pi_t = m_t + a_2 \tag{4.43}
$$

Now let us assume a very general partial adjustment mechanism so that we replace (4.43) with

$$
\pi_t = \epsilon(L) m_t + a_2. \tag{4.44}
$$

The rate of inflation in this model is equal to a constant plus a distributed lag in past money growth rates.

The rational expectation of inflation in this model would be formed by taking the expected value of (4.44), viz.,

$$\pi_t^* = \eta(L)m_{t-1} + a_2. \tag{4.45}$$

Market participants would form rational forecasts of inflation by gathering information on past rates of growth of the money stock and processing it as in (4.45). Suppose that forecasts are actually formed according to

$$\pi_t^* = \eta'(L)m_{t-1} + a_2'. \tag{4.46}$$

A test of the hypothesis that forecasts are formed rationally in this model is equivalent to a test of the hypothesis:

$$H_0 : \eta'(L) = \eta(L) \tag{4.47}$$

against the alternative hypothesis that they are not equal.

By steps similar to (4.25) through (4.28), above, we could shift (4.45) forward, apply Wold's chain principle of forecasting, and collect terms to get an expression for the rational expectation of inflation for period $t + 1$, π_{t+1}^*,

$$\pi_{t+1}^* = a_2 + \eta_1(L)m_{t-1}. \tag{4.48}$$

An investor would form the rational expectation of inflation π_{t+1}^*, by regressing actual rates of inflation on a distributed lag of past money growth and a constant,

$$\pi_{t+1} = a_2 + \eta_1(L)m_{t-1}. \tag{4.49}$$

Suppose forecasts are actually formed by the relation

$$\pi_{t+1}^* = a_2' + \eta_1'(L)m_{t-1}. \tag{4.50}$$

Combine (4.32) and (4.50) to get an expression for r_{t+1},

$$r_{t+1} = a_2' + \rho + \eta_1'(L)m_{t-1}. \tag{4.51}$$

Subtract (4.49) from (4.51) to get,

$$r_{t+1} - \pi_{t+1} = (a_2' + \rho - a_2) + [\eta_1'(L) - \eta'(L)]m_{t-1}. \tag{4.52}$$

If forecasts of inflation are formed rationally in this model the bracketed term on the r.h.s. of (4.52) will be approximately zero. We can reject the hypothesis of rationally formed expectations if the F-statistic for the regression (4.52) as a whole exceeds a suitable chosen critical value. Table 4-4 presents an estimate of (4.52); the F-statistic for the regression is of value $F = 0.44$, supporting the hypothesis that expectations, as revealed in market interest rates, are formed rationally.

The possible objection that both $\eta_1'(L)$ and $\eta_1(L)$ are zero should be answered. Estimates of these lag polynomials are presented, respectively, in Tables 4-5 and 4-6, and enter the regression with F-statistics of 30.26 and 11.03, respectively. This allows us to reject the hypotheses that $\eta_1'(L) = 0$ and that $\eta_1(L) = 0$, answering the criticism.

Table 4-4

Parameter Estimates of Equation (4.52),

$$r_{t+1} - \pi_{t+1} = (a_2' + \rho - a_2) + [\eta_1'(L) - \eta_1(L)]m_{t-1}$$

$$[\eta_1'(L) - \eta_1(L)]$$

t-1	.0602 (0.95)	$(a_2' + \hat{\rho} - a_2) = 1.7148$ (3.97)
t-2	.0262 (0.90)	$[\eta_1'(1) - \hat{\eta}_1(1)] = -.0629$ (0.50)
t-3	.0055 (0.22)	
t-4	−.0049 (0.18)	
t-5	−.0079 (0.31)	Statistics
t-6	−.0065 (0.29)	R^2 = 0.03
		SSE = 178.476
t-7	−.0037 (0.16)	N = 65
		D-W = 1.78
t-8	−.0023 (0.09)	
t-9	−.0054 (0.19)	
t-10	−.0160 (0.62)	
t-11	−.0369 (1.16)	
t-12	−.0712 (1.06)	

Notes: See notes to Table 3-1, Chapter 3. $[\eta_1'(L) - \eta_1(L)]$ satisfies a third-order polynomial with no endpoint restrictions.

Table 4-5
Parameter Estimates of Equation (4.51),

$$r_{t+1} = (a_2' + \rho) + \eta_1'(L)m_{t-1}$$

$\hat{\eta}_1'(L)$		
t-1	.0731	$(a_2' \overset{\wedge}{+} \rho) = 2.2709$
	(2.29)	(10.37)
t-2	.0667	$\eta_1'(1) = .6581$
	(4.52)	(10.50)
t-3	.0654	
	(5.31)	
t-4	.0673	
	(4.93)	
t-5	.0706	Statistics
	(5.53)	$R^2 = 0.67$
t-6	.0734	$SSE = 45.3694$
	(6.62)	$N = 65$
t-7	.0739	$D\text{-}W = 0.89$
	(6.45)	
t-8	.0703	
	(5.20)	
t-9	.0607	
	(4.19)	
t-10	.0432	
	(3.29)	
t-11	.0160	
	(1.00)	
t-12	−.0226	
	(0.67)	

Notes: See notes to Table 3-1, Chapter 3. $\eta_1'(L)$ satisfies a third-order polynomial with no endpoint restrictions.

Again it may be conjectured that the result is simply due to the strong assumption of the expectations theory of the term structure of interest rates; this is not so. I have also estimated a model using the three month Treasury Bill rate in the dependent variable. The relevant equation to estimate for the three month Treasury Bill rate, it should be clear, is

$$r_t - \pi_t = (a_2' + \rho - a_2) + (\eta'(L) - \eta(L))m_{t-1}. \tag{4.53}$$

The F-statistic for the estimate of (4.53) is $F = 0.85$. This provides additional evidence in favor of the hypothesis of rational expectations.

Table 4-6
Parameter Estimates of Equation (4.49),

$$\pi_{t+1} = a_2 + \eta_1(L)m_{t+1}$$

	$\hat{\eta}_1(L)$	
t-1	.0131	$\hat{a}_2$ = .4908
	(0.23)	(1.26)
t-2	.0424	$\hat{\eta}(1)$ = .7432
	(1.61)	(6.59)
t-3	.0627	
	(2.80)	
t-4	.0754	
	(3.02)	
t-5	.0816	Statistics
	(3.50)	R^2 = 0.42
t-6	.0826	SSE = 145.255
	(4.09)	N = 65
t-7	.0797	D-W = 1.67
	(3.87)	
t-8	.0742	
	(3.07)	
t-9	.0672	
	(2.61)	
t-10	.0600	
	(2.57)	
t-11	.0540	
	(1.89)	
t-12	.0503	
	(0.83)	

Notes: See notes to Table 3-1, Chapter 3. $\eta_1(L)$ satisfies a third-order polynomial with no endpoint restrictions.

4.5 Models with Autoregressive Real Rate

The real rate of interest may be viewed as the expected real rate of return on assets. It may be useful to examine a model in which the formation of these expectations is explicitly stated, rather than assume those expectations are static, or constant, as in the preceding analysis. We will choose one alternative model, that investors form expectations of the future real rate of return *by taking a weighted sum of previous realized real rates of return, that is, autoregressively.* This is of special interest because it has been used with apparent success in recent papers by Modigliani and Sutch[13] and Modigliani and Schiller.[14] The autoregressive specification may be written as

$$\rho_{t+i} = \omega_1\rho_{t-1} + \ldots + \omega_w\rho_{t-w}$$
$$= (1 + \omega_1 L + \ldots + \omega_w L^W)\rho_{t-1} = \omega(L)\rho_{t-1}. \tag{4.54}$$

But since $\rho_t = r_t - \pi_t$, we also have

$$\rho_{t+i} = \omega(L)r_{t-1} - \omega(L)\pi_{t-1}. \tag{4.55}$$

The latter was used by Modigliani and Schiller—hereafter M-S—in conjunction with an autoregressive specification for the expected rate of inflation. In an unpublished paper,[15] I have argued that M-S are guilty of the same type of specification error as the authors criticized in Chapter 3. The tests presented in this section will accordingly be aimed at two issues. (1) Incorporating the assumption (4.55) into an equation for nominal interest rates does not alter the conclusion of Chapter 3; autoregressive models of the formation of inflation expectations are misspecified. They omit variables related to realized rates of money growth. (2) Expectations of inflation estimated in this model assuming autoregressive real rate, are rational, providing further support for the test results presented in Section 4.4.

First we would like to incorporate (4.55) into an interest rate equation. Let $i = 1$ in (4.55) and substitute (4.55) and (4.30) into (4.32) to obtain

$$r_{t+1} = a_1' + \omega(L)r_{t-1} + [\delta_1'(L) - \omega(L)]\pi_{t-1} + \psi_1'(L)m_{t-1}. \tag{4.56}$$

Now it is clear that by operating on (4.25) by F^i—shifting forward i periods—applying Wold's chain principle recursively, and collecting terms, we can, in general, write for arbitrary $i > 0$,

$$\pi_{t+i}^* = a_1 + \delta_i(L)\pi_{t-1} + \psi_i(L)m_{t-1}. \tag{4.57}$$

This expresses the rational forecast of inflation in period $(t + i)$ as a function of realized values on money growth and inflation. Combining (4.57) and (4.55) and the Fisher relation for forward rates of interest,

$$r_{t+i} = \rho_{t+i} + \pi_{t+i}^*, \tag{4.58}$$

to obtain the expression for an arbitrary forward one-period rate of interest;

$$r_{t+i} = a_1' + \omega(L)r_{t-1} + [\delta_i'(L) - \omega(L)\pi_{t-1} + \psi_i'(L)m_{t-1}, \tag{4.59}$$

where the primes indicate that I am referring to actual expectations held by investors, which may not be equivalent to (4.57). M-S used an autoregressive assumption of the formation of expectations of inflation, similar to our assumption (3.18) of Chapter 3,

$$\pi_t^* = \tau(L)\pi_{t-1} + a_1. \tag{4.60}$$

By operating on (4.60) by F^i, applying the chain principle of forecasting, and collecting terms we can write, for arbitrary $i > 0$,

$$\pi_{t+i}^* = \tau_i(L)\pi_{t-1} + a_1'. \tag{4.61}$$

Substitute (4.55) and (4.61) into (4.58) to obtain the expression for the forward rate of interest for period $(t + i)$,

$$r_{t+i} = a_1' + \omega(L)r_{t-1} + [\tau_i(L) - \omega(L)]\pi_{t-1}, \tag{4.62}$$

under the hypothesis of autoregressive expectations of inflation.

In order to examine long rates of interest we will adopt an assumption of M-S which states that we can regard the n-period rate of interest, where n is large, as a weighted sum of future expected one-period rates of interest each of which are determined by (4.59) under the hypothesis of rational expectations of inflation, or (4.62) under the hypothesis of autoregressive expectations of inflation. From (4.59) we know that each expected one period rate of interest is the sum of (1) a weighted sum of past realized short rates of interest, (2) a weighted sum of past realized rates of inflation, and (3) a weighted sum of past realized rates of change of the money stock. We can express the long-rate of interest as a sum of three corresponding weighted sums, as follows;

$$R_{t+n} = b_1 + \Omega_n(L)r_{t-1} + \Delta_n(L)\pi_{t-1} + \Psi_n(L)m_{t-1}. \tag{4.63}$$

The model which we have developed from the assumption of rational forecasting implies, then, that we can explain the long rate of interest with information on past rates of interest, past rates of inflation, and past rates of change in the stock of money. The hypothesis of AE used by M-S leads to (4.63), with $\psi_n(L) = 0$. We are now in a position to test several interesting implications of our model against those of the model used by M-S, which is equivalent to (4.63), but with $\psi(L) = 0$.

If expectations are actually formed rationally then the model estimated by Modigliani and Schiller is misspecified due to the omission of the distributed lag on past money growth rates (i.e., $\Psi(L)$ in (4.63) and $\psi'(L)$ in (4.59)). Hence their model is equivalent to the hypothesis that $\Psi(L) = \psi_i'(L) = 0$ in our model, while rational expectations implies that these lags should be nonzero. Table 4-7 presents some statistics from estimates of the M-S specification as well as the specification suggested by our model of rational expectations. For the dependent variable we use U.S. data on five alternative nominal rates of interest. These are r_{t+1}, the three month Treasury Bill rate, the six month Treasury Bill rate, the rate on 4-6 month Prime Commercial Paper, and the rate on AAA Corporate Bonds. The F-statistics for the null hypothesis that $\psi_i(L) = 0 = \Psi(L)$ are as follows:

Table 4-7
Statistics from Estimates of Models Adopting the Autoregressive Real Rate Assumption (4.55)

Equation	Form Estimated	R^2	SSE	N	k	D-W	h
1a	$r_{t+1} = a'_1 + \omega(L)r_{t-1} + [\delta'(L)-\omega(L)]\pi_{t-1}$	.67	45.74	64	9	1.23	—
1b	$r_{t+1} = a'_1 + \omega(L)r_{t-1} + [\delta'(L)-\omega(L)]\pi_{t-1} + \psi'(L)m_{t-1}$	.80	27.99	65	13	1.51	—
2a	$6mTB = a'_1 + \omega(L)r_{t-1} + [\delta'(L)-\omega(L)]\pi_{t-1}$	.76	30.91	65	9	1.12	—
2b	$6mTB = a'_1 + \omega(L)r_{t-1} + [\delta'(L)-\omega(L)]\pi_{t-1} + \psi'(L)m_{t-1}$	.86	17.31	65	13	1.42	—
3a	$3mTB = a'_1 + \omega(L)r_{t-1} + [\delta'(L)-\omega(L)]\pi_{t-1}$	.82	22.46	65	9	1.10	4.68
3b	$3mTB = a'_1 + \omega(L)r_{t-1} + [\delta'(L)-\omega(L)]\pi_{t-1} + \psi'(L)m_{t-1}$	.90	12.14	65	13	1.45	2.95
4a	$PCP = a'_1 + \omega(L)r_{t-1} + [\delta'(L)-\omega(L)]\pi_{t-1}$	.85	24.05	65	9	1.05	4.47
4b	$PCP = a'_1 + \omega(L)r_{t-1} + [\delta'(L)-\omega(L)]\pi_{t-1} + \psi'(L)m_{t-1}$	.92	13.34	65	13	1.30	3.96
5a	$AAA = a'_1 + \omega(L)r_{t-1} + [\delta'(L)-\omega(L)]\pi_{t-1}$	.97	3.87	65	9	1.13	—
5b	$AAA = a'_1 + \omega(L)r_{t-1} + [\delta'(L)-\omega(L)]\pi_{t-1} + \psi'(L)m_{t-1}$	.98	2.37	65	13	1.56	—
6a	$r_{t+1} - \pi_{t+1} = (a'_1-a_1) + \omega(L)r_{t-1} + [\delta'(L)-\delta(L)-\omega(L)]\pi_{t-1} + [\psi'(L)-\psi(L)]m_{t-1}$	.20	144.02	65	13	2.10	—
6b	$r_{t+1} - \pi_{t+1} = (a'_1-a_1) + \omega(L) [r_{t-1}-\pi_{t-1}]$	.08	165.53	65	5	1.76	—
7a	$3mTB - \pi_t = (a'_1-a_1) + \omega(L)r_{t-1} + [\delta'(L)-\delta(L)-\omega(L)]\pi_{t-1} + [\psi'(L)-\psi(L)]m_{t-1}$	.28	117.00	65	13	1.92	n.a.
7b	$3mTB - \pi_t = (a'_1-a_1) + \omega(L) [r_{t-1}-\pi_{t-1}]$	.11	143.64	65	5	1.81	n.a.

Note: See Notes to Table 3-1. Chapter 3. k is the number of parameters estimated; h is Durbin's h-statistic used to test for serial correlation in models with lagged endogenous variables on the r.h.s., h is distributed $N(0,1)$ under the null hypothesis; the coefficients of all lag polynomials were constrained to satisfy third-order polynomials, with no zero restrictions on the endpoints; $3mTB$ is the three month Treasury Bill rate; $6mTB$ is the six month Treasury Bill rate; PCP is the rate on four to six month Prime Commercial Paper; AAA is the rate on AAA Corporate bonds; r_{t-1} is the lagged $3mTB$ rate in Equations 1a, 1b, 2a, 2b, 3a, 3b, 6a, 6b, and is the lagged PCP rate in Equations 4a, 4b, 5a, 5b, 7a, 7b; n.a. means "not applicable" and was used when Durbin's h-statistic was not calculable.

$F = 8.25$ for the r_{t+1} rate
$F = 11.05$ for the three month Treasury Bill rate
$F = 10.20$ for the six month Treasury Bill rate
$F = 10.43$ for the 4-6 month Prime Commercial Paper rate
$F = 8.25$ for the AAA Corporate Bond Rate.

The results uniformly confirm the hypothesis suggested by our model, that information on past money growth rates is incorporated into forecasts of inflation. We are led to conclude that a model which omits variables on money growth is misspecified. Further evidence in the importance of the money growth variables is provided by the reduction in serial correlation that occurs when these variables are added. Each of the Equations (Table 4-7) 1a, 2a, 3a, 4a, 5a, exhibits substantially higher Durbin-Watson statistic than its 1b, 2b, 3b, 4b, 5b counterpart. Omitted variables have apparently been found. Still, though, the D-W statistics of the "b" equations suggest that other variables which might appear in a more detailed model of inflation, or of real rates of interest, have been omitted.

We can go still deeper and test the hypothesis that the forecasts of inflation implied by our model are formed rationally by investors. This test is related to the test performed in Table 4-4 under the assumption of constant real rate of interest.

A rational investor will forecast inflation for period ($t + 1$) by estimating the parameters in (4.29). Now subtract (4.29) from (4.59)–with $i = 1$–to obtain

$$r_{t+1} - \pi_{t+1} = (a_1' - a_1) + \omega(L)r_{t-1}$$

$$+ [\delta_1'(L) - \delta(L)]\pi_{t-1} + [\psi_1'(L) - \psi_1(L)]m_{t-1}. \tag{4.64}$$

If forecasts of inflation are formed rationally then (4.34) holds and I can write (4.64) as

$$r_{t+1} - \pi_{t+1} = (a_1' - a_1) + \omega(L)[r_{t-1} - \pi_{t-1}]. \tag{4.65}$$

Thus we can test the hypothesis of rational expectations by estimating both (4.64) and (4.65), and then checking whether or not the restrictions imposed on the coefficients of (4.65) significantly increase the sum of squared residuals over those of (4.64). Equation 6a of Table 4-7 presents statistics from estimates of (4.64) while Equation 6b of Table 4-7 presents statistics from estimates of (4.65). The rate of interest in the dependent variable is r_{t+1}. All lag distributions are of order twelve; their coefficients are constrained to satisfy third-order polynomials, with no endpoint constraints. We will reject the hypothesis (4.34) of rational expectations if the value of the F-statistic exceeds a suitably chosen critical value. In fact, the F-statistic is of value $F = 0.968$; the evidence presented does not allow us to reject the hypothesis of rational expectations.

Equations 7a and 7b (Table 4-7) duplicate this test with one major change; the rate of interest in the dependent variable is the three month Treasury Bill rate. The test of the hypothesis of rational expectations, (4.34), using the three month Treasury Bill rate yields an F-statistic of value $F = 0.848$; we are not able to reject the hypothesis of rational expectations presented on the evidence presented in this study.

The results of tests performed under the assumption that the real rate of return is forecast autoregressively, then, are uniformly in favor of the hypothesis of rational expectations of inflation. This, when taken in combination with the tests performed in earlier sections under the assumption of constant real rate, and under two alternative models of inflation, makes a strong case for the hypothesis that expectations of inflation are, in fact, formed rationally.

4.6 Conclusions

In this chapter I have presented several models of the determination of the rate of interest and have used them to test the hypothesis of rational expectations. Under the hypothesis that the real rate of interest is constant, the rational expectations theory cannot be rejected in either the model derived from the simple quantity theory of money, or that derived from the standard textbook model. Specification of the rational forecast of inflation took explicit account of the structure of the model of inflation. In the last section these expectations were incorporated into a model of interest rate forecasting, as suggested by Modigliani and Schiller, under the assumption that the real rate of interest is formed as an autoregression of past realized rates of return. I compared this model with that of M-S, which assumed inflation to be forecast extrapolatively, and found that their treatment of forecasts of inflation led them to omit variables relating to money growth, introducing a specification error. Tests of the predictive power of these omitted variables confirmed this claim. I then performed tests of the hypothesis of rational expectations using the M-S view of the real rate of interest by comparing the structure of the process generating inflation and the structure of forecasts of inflation. The evidence presented was strongly in favor of rational expectations.

Based on evidence presented in this chapter I must challenge the conclusions of M-S that,

. . . past interest rates and prices are, in fact, the two main variables on which the United States market bases, directly or indirectly, its forecast of the future course of the short rate.[16]

Information on money growth rates should be added to the variables on which the United States market bases its forecast of the short rate of interest. Models which omit this source of information implicitly assume that information on money growth rates is too costly for investors to collect, an assumption which I have argued deserves explicit testing. Indeed, test results presented here indicate that this is not the case. A caveat, however, is in order. These results for interest determination still exhibit evidence of positive serial correlation, suggesting that there are other relevant variables which have been omitted from the model. Further work in the direction of specifying models of rational expectations of the real rate of return, and more elaborate models of inflation would seem indicated.

In the next chapter we will relax one of the assumptions concerning the stochastic behavior of the exogenous variables, allowing nonzero expected values. We will examine how people might come to predict the behavior of future money growth and the effects of such predictions on a number of economic magnitudes.

5 Announcement Effects and Rational Expectations

There is widespread belief that government officials can influence economic magnitudes by simply making public predictions about future values of the unemployment rate or the rate of inflation or some other *state variable.* Announcement Effects refer to the reaction of market participants to such announcements. Let there be an announcement concerning the future rate of inflation made by, say, the Chairman of the Federal Reserve Board. Traders will then incorporate this new information into their forecasts of inflation.

In a world of rational expectations, however, announcement effects take on a special meaning. Since rational forecasts are based on the structure of the process which generates the variable to be predicted, it is announcements concerning the future paths of those same exogenous processes which are relevant to those who wish to form forecasts. If, for instance, we find that the observed rate of inflation depends on the previous histories of monetary and fiscal variables, then market forecasters will try to glean information about the probable future paths of those variables to aid them in forecasting. Announcements of public officials will only be incorporated into forecasts if they influence forecasters' subjective probability distributions of future values of exogenous variables. A corollary of this is that official predictions of government authorities and public announcements other than those about the future paths of monetary and fiscal variables will have little or no impact on forecasts. Incomes policies designed to break the back of inflation by altering forecasts of inflation will, in such a world, probably be ineffective.

In previous chapters we have presented and tested a model of rational forecasting of inflation. In this chapter I extend the model of rational forecasting in order to analyze more directly the effects of public announcements on inflation forecasts. Such an analysis may furnish information to policy makers about the way in which their actions are monitored by market participants and how these actions are translated into forecasts of inflation. If policy makers become aware that overly erratic actions can breed "destabilizing" expectations (i.e., expectations which have perverse effects on stabilization efforts), they may decide to alter their behavior. Indeed, they may even be able to use this knowledge of the way in which forecasts are formed to behave in such a way as to generate a certain structure of expectations when this is deemed desirable. The latter point has special relevance for the debate over the feasibility of "twisting" the term to maturity structure of nominal interest rates. We will discuss this in some detail in Section 5.4.

73

Let us represent the average rate of inflation during period t by the reduced form equation:

$$\pi_t = \theta M_t + \gamma X_t + a_0, \tag{5.1}$$

where, as in Chapter 3, θ and γ are combinations of the parameters of the structural model from which (5.1) was derived. The exogenous variables M_t and $\left\{ X_t \right\}$ are stochastic processes driven, respectively, by the stochastic processes $\left\{ m_t \right\}$ and $\left\{ v_t \right\}$.

$$M_t = m_t + \phi_1 m_{t-1} + \ldots, + \phi_q m_{t-q} = \phi(L) m_t, \tag{5.2}$$

$$X_t = v_t + \xi_1 v_{t-1} + \ldots, + \xi_p v_{t-p} = \xi(L) v_t, \tag{5.3}$$

where, as before, L is the lag or backshift operator defined such that $L x_t = x_{t-1}$. We would now like to relax the properties of the processes $\left\{ m_t \right\}$ and $\left\{ v_t \right\}$ somewhat over those assumed in earlier chapters. We will not regard them as white noise processes. Rather, we will assume that they are serially uncorrelated, constant variance processes, but that the mean of the process can be nonzero. In fact, we assume a separate mean value for each prediction of future m_{t+i} and v_{t+i} values. Notationally, we express this as:

$$
\begin{aligned}
E(m_{t-i}) &= \overline{m}_{t-i} & i=0,-1,-2,\ldots \;, \\
&= m_{t-i} & i=1,\; 2,\ldots,q \;\;;
\end{aligned}
\tag{5.4}
$$

$$
\begin{aligned}
E(v_{t-i}) &= \overline{v}_{t-i} & i=0,-1,-2,\ldots \;, \\
&= v_{t-i} & i=1,\; 2,\ldots,p \;.
\end{aligned}
\tag{5.5}
$$

Past realizations of both processes, i.e., values prior to and including $t-1$, are nonstochastic in forming forecasts at time t, hence have zero variance. In predicting future values of the m's and the v's, however, the stochastic properties are such that the mean of the probability distribution shifts from one future period to the next. Separate information is used to determine each mean value. In our model the m's will represent percent rates of change in the supply of money in the appropriate period and the v's represent the percent rate of change in government spending, as in the models in Chapters 3 and 4. M_t then, stands for a distributed lag of rates of growth of the money supply in periods prior to t; and X_t stands for a distributed lag in rates of change in government spending in previous periods. The distributed lags are, respectively, of orders q and p, both finite. We can represent the rate of inflation in this model by the reduced form Equation (5.1) after substituting (5.2) and (5.3):

$$\pi_t = \theta\phi(L)m_t + \gamma\xi(L)v_t + a_0. \tag{5.6}$$

The rational expectation of inflation that would be formed by a forecaster with full knowledge of the structure of the economy and of the stochastic properties of the exogenous variables is obtained by taking expected values of (5.6);

$$\pi_t^* = E(\pi_t) = \theta\phi(L)E(m_t) + \gamma\xi(L)E(v_t) + a_0. \tag{5.7}$$

This, as in Chapter 4, is the rational forecast of inflation for period t made on the basis of information available in period $(t-1)$.

We would now like to examine rational forecasts of inflation for periods subsequent to t (i.e., $t+1, t+2, \ldots, t+k$) but still based only on information available in period $(t-1)$. Define the linear operator F, the Forward-Shift Operator, such that,

$$FX_t = L^{-1}X_t = X_{t+1}. \tag{5.8}$$

Now to examine the rate of inflation during period $(t+k)$ we operate on (5.6) successively by F, k times (or equivalently by F^k) to obtain,

$$\pi_{t+k} = \theta\phi(L)m_{t+k} + \gamma\xi(L)v_{t+k} + a_0. \tag{5.9}$$

Now by taking expected values of (5.9) we can define the rational expectation of inflation k periods hence, π_{t+k}^*, to be,

$$\pi_{t+k}^* = \theta\phi(L)E(m_{t+k}) + \gamma\xi(L)E(v_{t+k}) + a_0 \tag{5.10}$$

$$= \theta[E(m_{t+k}) + \phi_1 E(m_{t+k-1}) + \ldots + \phi_q E(m_{t+k-q})]$$

$$+ \gamma[E(v_{t+k}) + \xi_1 E(v_{t+k-1}) + \ldots + \xi_p E(v_{t+k-p})] + a_0$$

This is equivalent to:

$$\pi_{t+k}^* = \theta[1,\phi_1,\ldots,\phi_q]\begin{bmatrix} E(m_{t+k}) \\ \vdots \\ E(m_{t+k-q}) \end{bmatrix} + \gamma[1,\xi_1,\ldots,\xi_p]\begin{bmatrix} E(v_{t+k}) \\ \vdots \\ E(v_{t+k-p}) \end{bmatrix} + a_0$$

or more concisely:

$$\pi_{t+k}^* = \theta\Phi E(m) + \gamma\Xi E(v) + a_0. \tag{5.11}$$

Some of the elements of the vectors (m) and (v) from (5.11) are stochastic and others are predetermined. The number of predetermined elements in each vector is determined by the structure of the system, i.e., by the values of q and p (the orders of the respective lag polynomials in the exogenous disturbances) and by the length of the prediction horizon k. For example, if we are forecasting the rate of inflation in the distant future:

$$k - \max(q,p) \geqslant 0, \tag{5.12}$$

and if investors hold static forecasts of $E(m_{t+i}) = \overline{m}$ and $E(v_{t+i}) = \overline{v}$, for $i > 0$, then all of the elements of (m) and (v) that are relevant for forecasting π^*_{t+k} are stochastic, and in this model will be estimated as set out in (5.4) and (5.5), $\overline{m}$ and $\overline{v}$. This would lead to an expected value of inflation for period $t + k$ (and for all others periods in the future for which (5.12) holds of:

$$\pi^*_{t+k} = \theta\,\phi(L)\overline{m} + \gamma\xi(L)\overline{v} = \theta\overline{m}\sum_{i=0}^{q}\phi_i + \gamma\overline{v}\sum_{i=0}^{p}\xi_i \tag{5.13}$$

where we now treat L as a dummy variable and define $\phi_0 = \xi_0 = 1$.

For our model it is of some interest to *not* assume constant means for the processes $\{m_t\}$ and $\{v_t\}$. We will, rather, assume that forecasters make their guesses (construct subjective probability distributions) for future values of exogenous disturbances by gathering information about their likely future paths. If some of the exogenous disturbances are policy-determined, then the attitudes of the policy makers become a potential source of information to forecasters. More precisely, let $\overline{m}_{t+i}$ represent the mean of the probability distribution for m_{t+1} (a random variable). The average rate of inflation during period $t + k$ that would be expected by a rational forecaster (one with full knowledge of the structure of the economy and the stochastic properties of the disturbances) on the basis of information available in period $t - 1$ is:

$$\pi^*_{t+k} = \theta\,\phi(L)E(m_{t+k}) + \gamma\xi(L)E(v_{t+k})$$

$$= \theta\sum_{i=0}^{q}\phi_i\overline{m}_{t+k-i} + \gamma\sum_{i=0}^{p}\xi_i\overline{v}_{t+k-i} + a_0. \tag{5.14}$$

The rational expectation in such a model depends on the expected future paths of the exogenous disturbances.

Announcement effects in a world of rational forecasting now have meaning. When policy makers make statements concerning their future actions this generates information which forecasters, in turn, translate into expected future paths of policy variables (the m's and v's of our model). The result is revision of estimates of future inflation. For example, when the Fed announces a lowering of the discount rate this may be interpreted by forecasters to imply that the rate of growth of the money supply will be higher than anticipated; forecasts of inflation in future periods will be revised upward accordingly. Expectations of inflation in a model of rational expectations, then, are influenced by stabilization policies and also by market participants' beliefs about *future* stabilization policies. If policy makers concern themselves with these expectations and wish to take their influence on other economic variables into account, they must interpret the effects of their announcements on expectations of inflation in each future period.

Let us look at the problem confronting policy makers in another way. In our model with rational expectations it is pointless for the stabilization authorities to try to measure "the expected rate of inflation," as one would be led to do in a world of extrapolative or adaptive expectations. Forecasts, in our model, are not static. Instead there is a separate and well defined forecast of inflation for *each* period in the future based on (1) the past realized time paths of all the exogenous disturbances in the structural model for inflation, and (2) the stochastic properties of future values of the exogenous disturbances, including any information relevant to these properties which has been made available by the stabilization authorities in the guise of public announcements. We can represent these forecasts by plotting one-period rates of inflation against the length of the prediction horizon (k in our model) to get a curve representing the (marginal) term structure of forecasts of inflation at time $t - 1$ for future periods $t, t + 1, t + 2, \ldots$.

The curve in Figure 5-1 is a hypothetical time series of the expected rate of inflation in the future, given the information available to forecasters in period $t - 1$. It is a stochastic process equal to the sum of two moving average processes driven, respectively, by $\left\{ m_t \right\}$ and $\left\{ v_t \right\}$. It can assume a wide variety of shapes depending on the likely future course of the exogenous disturbances; only with static expectations for the exogenous variables will the curve be flat beyond a certain range.

In order for the stabilization authorities to obtain a measure of the expected rate(s) of inflation appropriate to their decisions, they must examine the theory appropriate to each question individually. If, for example, they are concerned with the unemployment-wage change tradeoff, they are asking questions about the behavior of participants in the labor market. Expectations of labor market participants would be the relevant ones for such an analysis. It may be concluded that the expected rate of inflation during the duration of the contract being negotiated is the relevant cost to laborers. This can then be found to be one of the values for π^* plotted in Figure 5-1 or an average of several of them.

For other questions, different horizons may be relevant. For example, to decide which measure of the expected rate of inflation to use when analyzing

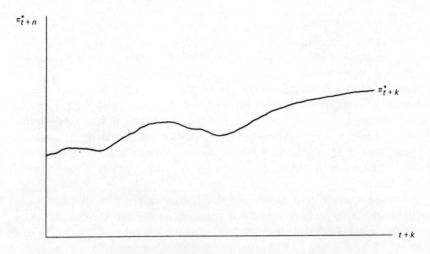

Figure 5-1. The Term Structure of π^*_{t+k}.

demand for money, we must ask ourselves what is the relevant cost of holding money. Friedman[1] argues that the effect of the expected rate of inflation ten periods in the future depends upon the fraction of our present money balances which we plan to still be holding during that period. Different answers to this question will yield different measures of the relevant expected rate of inflation for our analysis; each of which will be a weighted average of points in Figure 5-1. The interpretation of market rates of interest as indicators of monetary policy is another particularly important example of the need for a measure of *the* expected rate of inflation—one which has been responsible for a great deal of controversy among economists. In the remainder of this chapter we will analyze one aspect of this problem, that of twisting the term to maturity structure of interest rates.

5.1 Twisting the Term Structure

Although it occupies a prominent position in many writings on macroeconomics, the rate of interest is not a well defined concept in a real world economy. There is, conceptually, a rate of return associated with every asset in the economy. We can talk about the structure of yields of the entire spectrum of assets in terms of the characteristics of the assets which differentiate them in the minds of asset holders. One such characteristic which has long been discussed in economics literature is term to maturity. The term to maturity structure of interest rates concerns itself with yields on a spectrum of default-free securities differing only in term to maturity. The term structure at a point in time is typically summarized by the yield curve, which plots (nominal) rates of interest on the vertical axis and term to maturity on the horizontal axis. A hypothetical yield curve is shown in Figure 5-2. The yields relevant to the yield curve (the R_t's) are "long" or "spot" rates of interest. For example, R_{t+20} refers to the yield in today's market on a bond which will mature in period ($t + 20$).

Analysis of the term structure is important because we expect interest rates of securities with different maturities to play different roles in the economy. Theory suggests, for instance, that short rates play a major role in international capital flows and that long rates appear to be important in the determination of aggregate demand. Accordingly, it may be possible to promote national economic goals if policy makers have a way of influencing the term structure. In this section we will see what implications about the shape and position of the yield curve can be extracted from the models of forecasting that were developed in previous chapters. Our results will indicate that much of the controversy surrounding attempts of the Fed to twist the yield curve in the early nineteen sixties can be blamed on the failure to keep the distinction between nominal and real rates of interest in mind. We will conclude that twisting the yield curve is, indeed, feasible under a variety of assumptions about the real rate of interest; but that once this distinction is recognized, there is no longer a reason for undertaking such policies.

5.2 Operation Twist

Prior to 1961 the Federal Reserve System conducted their open-market operations almost entirely in the short-term Treasury Bill market. In other

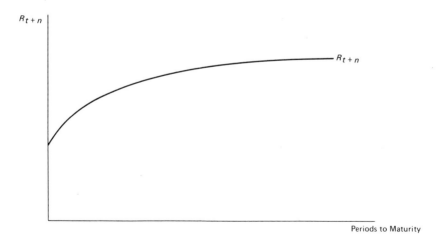

Figure 5-2. A Hypothetical Yield Curve.

words, they made no conscious attempt to alter the relationship between long and short term interest rates implicit in the yield curve. By 1960, however, concern over the balance of payments deficit led those in charge of monetary policies to reassess the "bills only" policy. It was thought that international capital flows would respond to changes in the short term rate of interest. The balance of payments deficit (which was characterized by heavy capital exports) could be palliated by stimulating short-term capital imports through open market sales, which would tend to raise the Treasury Bill rate. However, large open-market sales of Treasury Bills would have depressed aggregate demand for two reasons: (1) higher interest rates would have depressed spending on both investment and consumption goods, and (2) the money supply would decrease as a result of the open-market operation. The Federal Reserve System found this to be unacceptable. In late 1960 and early 1961 the United States was at the low phase of a business recession following the negative monetary growth in (both narrow and broad) money during the last half of 1959 and the first half of 1960. To decrease the money supply further would have had perverse effects on aggregate demand.

Operation Twist was an attempt to use monetary policy to stimulate capital imports without sacrificing domestic stabilization goals. If it were feasible to engage in actions which would simultaneously raise the short rate and lower the long rate (or at least prevent it from rising), while not causing a fall in the supply of money, then both goals might be achieved together. If there were no connection between the market for long assets and that for short assets (i.e., if it were empirically true that cross price elasticities of demand between assets of different maturities were close to zero) then the solution is evident; increase the supply of short-term securities and decrease the supply of long-term securities. This would result in a clockwise twist of the yield curve.

The viability of policies designed to twist the yield curve by switching assets of different maturities in government portfolios depends on the applicability of the segmented markets hypothesis, a hypothesis about the preferences of asset holders with respect to maturity. If all asset holders were restricted, either by institutional constraints or by the properties of their preference maps, to hold assets of a limited range of maturities, then changes in yields on assets of alternative maturities would not alter their behavior. This hypothesis implies that the demand curve for, say, twenty-year-bonds will not shift substantially due to a change in the yield on Treasury Bills; or that the demand for bonds of a given maturity is quite inelastic with respect to the price of bonds of different maturity.

A weaker hypothesis of the behavior of asset holders, the Preferred Habitat Theory, states that investors *prefer* to hold assets within a certain (narrow) range of maturities. Some large asset holders are restricted by law in the distribution of maturities of their assets; others may be willing to pay a premium for assets of certain maturities because they provide a hedge against changes in the value of certain of their liabilities; others may simply operate on a particular range of the yield curve because they have acquired some expertise in collecting and assimilating information about these assets, and not about others. *If* asset markets are dominated by large investors with "preferred habitats" for maturities, and *if* there is no speculative element in the asset markets large enough to give the yield curve continuity, then twisting the yield curve can be accomplished in the manner presented above, by altering the relative supplies of assets with open-market operations.

Testing the viability of twisting the yield curve involves estimating the properties of demand functions for assets of a given maturity, and looking at the magnitude of the estimated cross-elasticities of demand with respect to the prices (or yields) of assets of other maturities. Although there have been several attempts to gather evidence on this issue,[2] the results have not been conclusive for the United States experience in the early 1960s. It is not my intent to undertake such a test in this study. Rather, I wish to examine the implications of a rival theory of the term structure of interest rates, the expectations theory, concerning the feasibility of twisting the yield curve. These implications are of interest precisely because they differ greatly from those claimed by many adherents of the Expectations Theory. The key to the controversy will be seen to be the distinction between real and nominal rates of interest and the introduction of rational forecasting on the part of asset holders.

We shall develop the Expectations Theory in its purest form, the "unbiased" expectations theory. This theory assumes away risk and uncertainty along with liquidity considerations; the cost of such bold assumptions is justified here by the increased simplicity of exposition.

Consider an investor who has decided to loan a certain sum of money (make an investment) for, say, ten years. In a world of perfect certainty, where all information can be collected and used costlessly, and where there are zero transactions costs associated with making investments, the only important feature for the investor is the rate of return. If there are several alternative ways of "packaging" the same investment (i.e., a given size loan for a given period) then the investor will always choose the "package" which offers the highest rate of return. An investor who wishes to lend a sum of money for ten years, for example, can pursue a wide variety of options.[a] The most obvious is that he can buy a ten year bond and hold it to maturity. But he can also buy a twenty year bond with the anticipation of selling the bond at the end of ten years and realizing a capital gain. He can buy a five year bond, hold it to maturity, and then reinvest the proceeds in a similar instrument which will be held to maturity. Alternatively, he can form an investment plan in which he purchases one-year bonds, holds them to maturity, then uses the proceeds at maturity to purchase additional one-year bonds, and so forth for a ten year period. Clearly, in this

---

[a]Here we assume there are no "lumpy" investment constraints on the investor's behavior, i.e., bonds of any maturity value can be purchased or sold.

certainty model, the investor will choose the investment plan that yields the highest return. Opportunities for arbitrage, then, will assure us that the yield on all possible investment plans for this same ten-year investment will tend to equality. In other words, in this certainty model we have the following relationship between the rate of return on an n-period investment and the rates of return on one-period investments which are forecast by market traders today:

$$(1 + R_{t+n})^{n+1} = (1 + r_t)(1 + r_{t+1}) \ldots (1 + r_{t+n}), \qquad (5.15)$$

where R_{t+n} is the (spot) rate of interest prevailing in the market today for an ($n + 1$)-period bond, r_t ($= R_t$) is the interest rate on one-period bonds in today's market (which is also the one period expected rate of interest, for period t) and r_{t+n} is the rate of interest expected by the traders in today's market on a one-period loan that matures ($n + 1$) periods in the future.

The validity of (5.15) for a certainty model is obvious; expected future short-term rates of interest are known today and are equal to actual future short-term rates of interest. Investors would choose the form of a given investment solely on the expected (i.e., the actual yield of the investment. Intertemporal arbitrage would assure the validity of (5.15): if the long-rate of (5.15) were too high, then investors could borrow funds in the short-term loan market and use them to buy long-term bonds which they would hold to maturity. At the beginning of the next period the short-term loan could be retired by borrowing again in the short market. In this manner investors would make a certain profit. The arbitrage activities would drive up the price of long-term bonds, lowering their yield until (5.15) was again satisfied and opportunities for arbitrage would no longer exist.

The Expectations Hypothesis of the term structure of interest rates claims that investors' preferences are such that this certainty model can be usefully applied to real world interest rate determination. It says that we can usefully regard the term to maturity structure of interest rates as being determined by the expected path of future short-term interest rates as represented by (5.15). In other words, uncertainty about this future path of short-term interest rates has no systematic effect on the structure of rates.

The essence of the Expectations Theory, then, is that there is a great deal of continuity in the yield curve; in other words, the market for assets of a given maturity is closely linked to the markets for assets of all other maturities. It follows that attempts to alter the relationship between short and long term interest rates by varying the relative supplies of assets within these maturities are doomed to failure. The demand for assets of different maturities depends on the existing structure of interest rates; any change in these rates which disrupts the normal relationship (5.15) will result in accommodating shifts in demand and a new equilibrium price vector satisfying (5.15).

Those who accept the expectations theory have looked skeptically at the twisting policies pursued by the Fed in the 'sixties. Meiselman's path-breaking study in 1961,[3] interpreted as evidence in favor of the expectations theory, contributed to the skepticism among economists over the feasibility of twisting.[b] We will take a closer look at this possibility. When we look at twisting in a model with rational expectations and which recognizes both the Expectations Theory and the Fisher relation, the result will be that twisting the yield curve is, indeed, quite feasible. Moreover, if the shape and position of the yield curve are matters of importance to policy-makers, then the effects of stabilization policies and announcements concerning future stabilization policies[c] on the yield curve must be weighed in decision making.

5.3 "Twisting" and Rational Expectations

The conclusions of this model will rest on the tenability of the empirical assumptions upon which it is constructed. We will assume that:

1. The Expectations Theory in its purest form can usefully represent interest rate determination.
2. The Fisher Relation that $r = \rho + \pi^*$ (over the relevant time period) is always satisfied.
3. Individual forecasters form their predictions rationally (in the sense discussed in Chapter 4). This implies that they monitor the actions and announcements of those who control the exogenous disturbances in the economy.

The first assumption allows us to view spot rates of interest (the rates of interest observed in the market on ($n + 1$) periods bonds maturing ($n + 1$) periods in the future) as the geometric average of ($n + 1$) consecutive one-period forces of interest[d] expected to prevail in the future on the basis of information available today, minus one. This may be summarized by reproducing (5.15).

$$(1 + R_{t+n})^{n+1} = (1 + r_t)(1 + r_{t+1}) \ldots (1 + r_{t+n}). \tag{5.16}$$

Here r_{t+n} is to be interpreted as the one-period rate of interest that investors expect to prevail during period ($t + n$) on the basis of information available in period $t - 1$. A similar relationship exists for n-period interest rates:

[b]For example, Paul Samuelson recently remarked; "within limits changes in the composition of Fed purchases as between short bills and long bonds can slightly influence the shape of the yield differentials between long- and short-term assets. But apparently only within narrow limits unless massive 'twists' are indulged in.[4]

[c]More exactly the exogenous disturbances entering the reduced form equation for the rate of inflation and the real rate of interest.

[d]The force of interest is defined to be $(1 + r)$ where r is the relevant nominal rate of interest.

$$(1 + R_{t+n-1})^n = (1 + r_t)(1 + r_{t+1}) \ldots (1 + r_{t+n-1}).$$ (5.17)

Since the theory of rational expectations was presented in previous chapters in terms of one-period rates of inflation, we would like to choose a corresponding method of exposition for the term structure. We can use (5.16) and (5.17) to get:

$$\frac{(1 + R_{t+n})^{n+1}}{(1 + R_{t+n-1})^n} = (1 + r_n),$$ (5.18)

which allows us to calculate forward one-period rates of interest implicit in the term to maturity structure of interest rates. The R_{t+n} are determined in the spot loan market; r_{t+n} represents the rate of interest on a one-period bond which will mature in period n which must be expected by investors in order for (5.16) to hold; i.e., in order that there exist no opportunities for intertemporal arbitrage in this market.

Given a certain structure of the R_{t+n}, then we can calculate the entire structure of the r_{t+n} in the manner shown in (5.18). It follows that corresponding to a given yield curve (the geometric representation of the term structure of interest rates) there is a curve, the abscissa of which is term to maturity and the ordinate of which is the expected one-period rate of interest (i.e., the implicit forward rate of interest). We shall call this the "marginal yield curve." In Figure 5-3 we present a hypothetical yield curve and its corresponding marginal yield curve as an example of this relationship. Since the marginal yield curve is simply

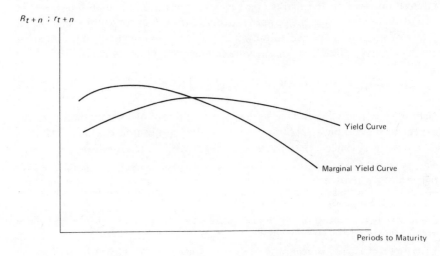

Figure 5-3. A Yield Curve and the Corresponding Marginal Yield Curve.

an alternative presentation of the same information contained in a yield curve, we can conveniently conduct our analysis in terms of the former without loss of generality. The relationship between the curves in Figure 5-3 is similar to that between an average revenue curve and a marginal revenue curve. If the (average) yield curve is rising with term to maturity, this implies that the marginal yield curve lies above it in this range. If the yield curve is falling with term to maturity, this implies that the marginal yield curve lies below it in this range.

We will now decompose the marginal yield curve into the sum of two related curves by acknowledging the Fisher Relation. We will assume that the Fisher Relation is valid for any time period:

$$R_{t+n} = \rho + \pi^*. \tag{5.19}$$

The nominal rate of interest for a given maturity bond will equal the real rate of interest plus the average rate of inflation expected to prevail, both defined over the time period relevant to the bond. This relationship generalizes straightforwardly to expected or forward rates of interest:

$$r_{t+n} = \rho_{t+n} + \pi^*_{t+n}. \tag{5.20}$$

The one-period rate of interest expected to prevail ($n + 1$) periods in the future is equal to the real rate of interest in that period plus the average rate of inflation expected over that period. In Figure 5-4, we plot ρ_{t+n} against term to maturity and define the real marginal yield curve to represent the real rate of interest on one-period bonds which mature ($n + 1$)-periods in the future. By

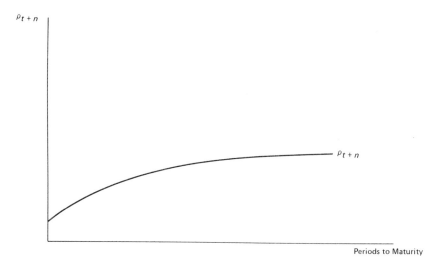

Figure 5-4. A Real Marginal Yield Curve.

summing the expected inflation schedule of Figure 5-1 and the marginal real yield curve of Figure 5-4, we get the marginal yield curve of Figure 5-3; this is shown in Figure 5-5.

A shift in the yield curve implies a change in the marginal yield curve. This can either be because there has been a change in the real marginal yield curve of Figure 5-4, or because investors have altered their forecasts of inflation for future periods. We recall that in a world of rational forecasts of inflation we have Equation (5.14),

$$\pi_{t+k}^* = \theta \phi(L)E(m_{t+k}) + \gamma \xi(L)E(v_{t+k}) + a_0,$$

$$= \theta \sum_{i=0}^{q} \phi_i \overline{m}_{t+k-i} + \gamma \sum_{i=0}^{p} \xi_i \overline{v}_{t+k-i} + a_0. \qquad (5.21)$$

In other words, the rate of inflation forecast for any future period will depend on investors' forecasts of the future paths (or the expected values of these future paths) of the exogenous processes which enter the reduced-form equation for inflation. Thus the "term structure" of expected inflation, as shown in Figure 5-1, depends on these same forecasts about the exogenous processes. Changes in the subjective probability distributions of investors concerning these processes will result in a shift of the term structure of inflation forecasts, hence in a change in the marginal yield curve, implying a corresponding change in the yield curve. If some of the exogenous processes are controlled by policy makers, then

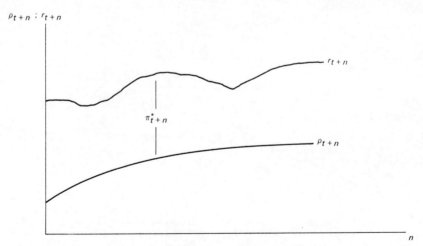

Figure 5-5. A Set of Real and Nominal Marginal Yield Curves.

forecasts of inflation may be altered by announcements to investors about future policy actions, much in the way discussed in the early sections of this chapter.

We are now in a position to discuss the feasibility of twisting the yield curve. We will assume a given structure of real rates of interest, hence a given real marginal yield curve, for this analysis. This does not mean that we are assuming that real rates of interest do not change, but rather, that at a point in time investors hold forecasts about the future course of the real rate of return, and that these forecasts will not be altered by announcements concerning the likely future course of the exogenous disturbances in the reduced-form equation for inflation.[e]

Given a real marginal yield curve, the marginal yield curve is determined by the term structure of inflation forecasts. Actions of the stabilization authorities affect forecasts of inflation by influencing investors' subjective probability distributions of the future course of exogenous disturbances. This implies that the marginal term structure of interest rates also depends on the same exogenous disturbances and can also be influenced by actions of the stabilization authorities. If policy makers announce future paths of all disturbances under their control, e.g., the rates of change of the money supply and of government spending—and if we assume that investors believe the announcements—then they can generate a corresponding term structure of forecasts of one-period rates of inflation. Given knowledge of the real marginal yield curve, then, the monetary authorities can announce future paths of all exogenous disturbances under their control, in ways that will generate marginal yield curves of many possible configurations. They can alter the relationship between long and short rates of interest by controlling the information that is fed into investors' inflation forecasting mechanisms.

5.4 Achieving a "Target" Yield Curve

We will now look at the problem facing the monetary authorities in greater detail. Let the monetary authorities decide, for whatever reason, that a certain term structure of nominal interest rates would further their policy efforts. This implies a target yield curve which we will denote:

---

[e]Actually this assumption is stronger than need be imposed to achieve the results we desire. We have, in effect, assumed orthogonality between real rates of interest and the exogenous disturbances controlled by the stabilization authorities. All that is necessary for the following analysis is that the effects on the one-period forecast of inflation dominate the effects on the marginal real rate of interest for each future period. In other words, if there is a change in the growth rate of the money stock, then we require that the change in the forecast of inflation (measured in basis points) be strictly larger than the change in the real rate of interest (also measured in basis points) due to the monetary action. As an empirical matter, the effect of monetary actions on the real rate of interest is not, in any case, clearly established.

$$R'_n = \begin{bmatrix} R'_t \\ R'_{t+1} \\ . \\ . \\ . \\ R'_{t+s} \end{bmatrix} \tag{5.22}$$

where $(t + s)$ represents the period of maturity of the longest instrument outstanding, or the longest about which the authorities are concerned. The first step in trying to implement policies to achieve (5.22) is to translate the yield curve implicit in (5.22) into the corresponding marginal yield curve. Marginal, or forward, rates of interest are calculated from (5.22) by:

$$r'_{t+n} = \frac{(1 + R'_{t+n})^{n+1}}{(1 + R_{t+n-1})^n} - 1.0, \tag{5.23}$$

where n goes from zero to s. This yields the target marginal yield curve,

$$r'_n = \begin{bmatrix} r'_t \\ r'_{t+1} \\ . \\ . \\ . \\ r'_{t+s} \end{bmatrix} \tag{5.24}$$

We assume that the monetary authorities face a given term structure of real interest rates, hence a given real marginal yield curve summarized in:

$$\bar{\rho}_{t+1} = \begin{bmatrix} \bar{\rho}_t \\ \bar{\rho}_{t+1} \\ . \\ . \\ . \\ \bar{\rho}_{t+s} \end{bmatrix} \tag{5.25}$$

which will not be altered by their policies. The monetary authorities are also aware of the process by which market participants form forecasts of inflation for future periods, i.e., they possess knowledge of the form and the coefficients of (5.21). We now restate the relationship among real rates of interest, nominal rates of interest, and forecasts of inflation:

$$
\begin{bmatrix} \bar{p}_t \\ \bar{p}_{t+1} \\ \cdot \\ \cdot \\ \cdot \\ \bar{p}_{t+s} \end{bmatrix}
+
\begin{bmatrix} \pi_t^* \\ \pi_{t+1}^* \\ \cdot \\ \cdot \\ \cdot \\ \pi_{t+s} \end{bmatrix}
=
\begin{bmatrix} r_t \\ r_{t+1} \\ \cdot \\ \cdot \\ \cdot \\ r_{t+s} \end{bmatrix}
\qquad (5.26)
$$

The job remaining for the monetary authorities to achieve the chosen term structure is to pick the correct "announcements." The correct announcements concerning the future paths of the exogenous disturbances are those which through (5.21) will result in the structure of forecasts of inflation needed to make the right-hand side of (5.26) equal to (5.24). But from (5.21) forecasts of inflation are formed by:

$$
\begin{bmatrix} \pi_t^* \\ \pi_{t+1}^* \\ \cdot \\ \cdot \\ \cdot \\ \pi_{t+s}^* \end{bmatrix}
= \theta
\begin{bmatrix} \bar{m}_t & m_{t-1} & \cdots & m_{t-q} \\ \bar{m}_{t+1} & \bar{m}_t & \cdots & m_{t-q+1} \\ \cdot & \cdot & & \cdot \\ \cdot & \cdot & & \cdot \\ \cdot & \cdot & & \cdot \\ \bar{m}_{t+s} & \bar{m}_{t+s-1} & \cdots & \bar{m}_{t+s-q} \end{bmatrix}
\begin{bmatrix} \phi_0 \\ \phi_1 \\ \cdot \\ \cdot \\ \cdot \\ \phi_q \end{bmatrix}
+
$$

$$
\gamma
\begin{bmatrix} \bar{v}_t & v_{t-1} & \cdots & v_{t-p} \\ \bar{v}_{t+1} & \bar{v}_t & \cdots & v_{t-p+1} \\ \cdot & \cdot & & \cdot \\ \cdot & \cdot & & \cdot \\ \cdot & \cdot & & \cdot \\ \bar{v}_{t+s} & \bar{v}_{t+s-1} & \cdots & \bar{v}_{t-p+s} \end{bmatrix}
\begin{bmatrix} \xi_0 \\ \xi_1 \\ \cdot \\ \cdot \\ \cdot \\ \xi_p \end{bmatrix}
+ a_0.
\qquad (5.27)
$$

Realized values of the m's and v's (e.g., m_{t-1}) are known both to the authorities and to investors and are regarded as parameters. Future m's and v's (e.g., $\overline{m}_t$), however, refer to values of the exogenous disturbances that have not yet taken place. This means that estimates of these variables by investors are subject to influence by the announcements of the authorities.

The problem facing the stabilization authorities, then, can be regarded as announcing future paths of $\left\{ m_t \right\}$ and $\left\{ v_t \right\}$ (which we assume will be adopted by investors as the expected value of probability distributions of these disturbances) in a way such that:

$$(5.27) = (5.24) - (5.25), \qquad\qquad (5.28)$$

i.e., such that the resulting marginal term structure is the target marginal yield curve of identity (5.24).

The system of equations represented by (5.27) is recursive in each exogenous process. This means that, in general, any desired marginal term structure (hence any desired term structure) can be achieved by an appropriate choice of the future paths of the exogenous disturbances. We will illustrate this as follows: Given any set of values for the future v's, those who control the $\left\{ m_t \right\}$ process can achieve any marginal term structure by first picking the value of $\overline{m}_t$ necessary to generate r_t', from (5.24). This value now becomes a parameter in their choice of the policy that will generate r_{t+1}', which they can now generate by the appropriate choice of $\overline{m}_{t+1}$. By proceeding in this manner they can solve for each value of $\overline{m}_{t+i}$, as i goes from 0 to s. Thus, given the behavior of the v's, a unique solution for the future path of the m's exists.

It is equally true that given a set of values for the $\overline{m}_{t+i}$ a unique solution for the v_{t+i} process exists because the second term of (5.27) is recursive in $\overline{v}_t$, $\overline{v}_{t+1}, \ldots, \overline{v}_{t+s}$. The stabilization authorities in charge of the exogenous process $\left\{ v_t \right\}$ can achieve, in this model, any marginal yield curve (hence any yield curve) by choosing the appropriate set of announcements.

If the authorities can vary both the $\left\{ m_t \right\}$ and the $\left\{ v_t \right\}$ process, then they have a wider variety of options. They can set the future behavior of one of the processes in the manner discussed above, then choose the appropriate set of announcements concerning the future paths of the other process to achieve the desired structure of interest rates. Or they can choose from (an infinite number of) mixed policies in which both the $\left\{ m_t \right\}$ process and the $\left\{ v_t \right\}$ process are announced to generate forecasts of inflation. The latter policy would, of course, allow more flexibility. It is likely, however, that the $\left\{ m_t \right\}$ process and the $\left\{ v_t \right\}$ process are important for other policy goals, so the choice of which of the particular combinations to use cannot be determined with reference to the term structure of interest rates alone.

5.5 Conclusions

We see, then that "twisting" the term structure of interest rates is not precluded by the expectations hypothesis. Indeed, it is the natural consequence of this hypothesis of the term structure of interest rates, once we introduce rational forecasting of inflation. At a point in time *any* yield curve can be generated in this model by the release of the appropriate information to those in the market. This is done by generating a desired structure of forecasts of inflation on the part of investors. At this point certain caveats are in order.

The link between announcements of the stabilization authorities and the subjective probability distributions of investors concerning the future behavior of the exogenous disturbances in this model has been assumed to be very simple. The authorities simply "announce" the future paths of these variables and investors believe them (shift their probability distributions to the announced mean). This assumption is tenuous at best. In the real world this could only continue as long as the authorities lived up to their announcements. They must actually perform the policies they announce to keep the faith of investors. This also implies that when the authorities generate a certain structure of forecasts of inflation, this is also the structure of the best estimates of future inflation. The costs of generating the inflation must be taken into account when calculating a policy of twisting the yield curve.

Even though a given yield curve can always be generated at a point in time by influencing forecasts of inflation, this does not imply that such a yield curve can be maintained over a succession of time periods. To do so would necessitate new announcements concerning the future behavior of the exogenous processes which would likely destroy the credibility of the stabilization authorities' announcements.

The result that twisting the yield curve is feasible in this model has little to do with the efforts of the Federal Reserve System in the early 'sixties. They tried to alter the structure of real rates of interest by changing relative supplies of assets of different maturities, without considering forecasts of inflation. We have concerned ourselves solely with forecasts of inflation and have assumed a constant structure of real rates of interest. The obvious implication is that the type of twisting in our model is worthless for stimulating aggregate demand by lowering interest rates, since real rates are certainly the relevant ones for investment decisions. The use of twisting to alter short-term capital flows, however, is consistent with our analysis. The nominal rate of interest is the relevant rate of return to a foreign investor who does not anticipate a change in exchange rates during the period of the investment, and the nominal rate *can* be altered by the type of announcements considered here.

As a closing note, I must emphasize that I am not advocating the *active manipulation of forecasts* by regulating the information that is leaked to investors. Likewise, I am not arguing that a policy of twisting is desirable in any sense. Indeed, as I have outlined above, in this model there are definite costs (future inflation) in such an approach, and little to be gained from twisting. On another level, until we accumulate much more information on the determination of the real rate of interest, there are severe risks involved with twisting. The advisability of using a particular policy is, in any case, a separate and distinct issue from the possibility of employing certain policies and the likely effects of such policies if they were to be employed. It is to the latter issue, the *theoretical question of feasibility*, to which I have addressed the analysis of this chapter.

The point to retain from this chapter is not that we are able to twist the yield curve. It is rather that the term structure must be interpreted very carefully due to the likely effects of official actions on the structure of interest rates. Identification of market interest rates with real rates can be very misleading.

We have endeavored to analyze the term structure in a model of rational expectations of the future rate of inflation, an area much neglected in monetary economics. As Meiselman stated:

I should think that in the huge amount of research on term structure, perhaps the greatest single deficiency has been the lack of clear distinction between real and nominal rates. One of the areas for fruitful research in the future is to make that distinction clearer by bringing prices and price expectations into the analysis explicitly.[5]

When we give explicit recognition to these points, we arrive at some very interesting results concerning the term structure. Our work, however, has been entirely analytic. Much work remains to be done in identifying and measuring the particular announcements which are important to investors in formulating their probabilistic statements concerning future stabilization policies.

6 Conclusions

The analysis of this book concerns the way in which market traders form anticipations of the future rate of inflation. The thesis is that existing empirical work on this question suffers from a serious defect. Whereas usual forecasting models are purely autoregressive, I contend that investors process additional types of information; empirical work presented in this study supports this claim.

I will now summarize the analysis of the preceding chapters, present the form of the hypotheses tested, and indicate some of the more important empirical results. The results will be compared to available alternatives in the literature. Implications of the results for policy will be examined and, finally, an attempt will be made to predict the most profitable areas for future research.

Economists recognize that expected inflation plays an important role in the determination of several key macroeconomic variables; theories of the rate of unemployment and of the market rate of interest include expected inflation as explanatory variables. Proper evaluation of stabilization policies requires understanding the effects of expected inflation, and requires empirical estimates of the magnitude of such effects.

A large amount of research has, in the past decade, been directed toward estimation of the effects of expected inflation on other variables, and toward testing alternative hypotheses about the way in which investors choose to form expectations of inflation. The model of forecast formation typically adopted by researchers is autoregressive; investors form forecasts of inflation by examining the serial correlation properties of the series of past realized rates of inflation. Other sources of information which could be exploited by investors are seldom incorporated into explicit formulations of forecasting models.

An explicit model of forecasting is presented in Chapter 3, focusing on the costs of and the returns to information used in forecasting. Under certain assumptions concerning the structure of information costs, a rational investor will, indeed, form predictions of future inflation autoregressively. In the general case, however, other types of information will also be collected and processed. In this model, then, autoregressive forecasting schemes implicitly assume a certain structure of information costs. Economies of scale in forecasting suggest that investors will process multiple sources of information in forecasting.

If investors actually process multiple sources of information, all autoregressive models of forecast formation are misspecified. Empirical work based on autoregressive models will, in this case, generally suffer from biased and inconsistent estimates of all parameters in the model. Thus it is important to test the hypothesis that forecasts are formed autoregressively against alternative, more general, models which allow incorporation of other types of information into forecasts of inflation. The most obvious candidate for other types of information is the behavior of the money supply. Evidence presented in Chapter 2 shows that this hypothesis is not a new one.

In Chapter 2 evidence is presented that both Keynes and Marshall recognized the influence of monetary policy on expectations of inflation. Subsequent treatments of expectations forecasting by rational profit maximizing investors are also summarized. Papers by John F. Muth[1], A.A. Walters,[2] and Charles R. Nelson[3] are interpreted as a continuation of the work of Keynes and Marshall: they are recognized as the logical predecessors of this study.

Chapter 2 also presents evidence concerning reasons for the unquestioned acceptance of autoregressive models in existing empirical work. I argue that misinterpretation of empirical results presented by Irving Fisher[4] is largely to blame. Fisher was concerned with the total relation between the rate of inflation and the nominal rate of interest. This led Fisher to regress the nominal rate of interest on a distributed lag of past rates of inflation. He interpreted the relation partly in terms of expected inflation, but largely due to the *indirect* effects of inflation on real rates of interest (similar to those of the Wicksellian cumulative process). Subsequent writers on expectations have overlooked this point, and treated Fisher's analysis as one based solely on expected inflation. This led to the widespread adoption of autoregressive models of forecast formation, and to the premature presumption that lags in forming expectations are extremely long. Alternative sources of information were assumed too costly to be used by investors, hence not reflected in the market rate of interest.

Chapter 3 presents results of testing the hypothesis that predictions of inflation are formed autoregressively against the alternative hypothesis that they also incorporate information on past money growth rates. Section 3.1 presents a model of investor behavior in which the investor is assumed to maximize a two-period utility function $U(c_1,c_2)$ where the arguments are, respectively, levels of real consumption in period 1 and period 2. The investor faces given incomes in periods 1 and 2 and given initial assets, a given market rate of interest, and given costs and returns to information processing. He must choose the optimal level of period 1 consumption—implying the size of the portfolio invested until period 2—and the optimal level of the information processing activity. The solution exhibits economies of scale in forecasting; the optimal level of forecasting is directly related to the size of the portfolio. This suggests that by forming joint forecasts investors will utilize a larger subset of available information than the subset which would be used if forecasts were produced individually. Thus, on a priori grounds, we might expect forecasts reflected in market prices to be quite sophisticated if transactions costs are not prohibitive for joint forecasting.

Section 3.2 of Chapter 3 specifies the hypotheses to be tested. We present a simple macroeconomic model in which the rate of inflation is determined by distributed lags in both rates of money growth and rates of change in government spending. In symbols, we assume

$$\pi_t = \theta \phi(L) m_t + \gamma \xi(L) v_t + a_0, \tag{6.1}$$

where $\phi(L)$ and $\xi(L)$ are lag distributions of finite order, θ and γ are constants, m_t is the rate of money growth in period t, and v_t is the rate of change of government spending in period t. Under certain conditions on the roots of $\xi(L)$ and on the stochastic properties of the processes $\{m_t\}$ and $\{v_t\}$, we are able to conclude that an investor who knows the structure of (6.1) will forecast inflation by incorporating information on past inflation and on past money growth. Thus we obtain the expression

$$\pi_t^* = \delta(L) \pi_{t-1} + \psi(L) m_{t-1} + a_1, \tag{6.2}$$

where π_t^* denotes the rate of inflation in period t anticipated in period $t - 1$. I call the hypothesis (6.2) "consistent expectations," since the forecasts are consistent with the structure of the process generating inflation.

The null hypothesis, that forecasts of inflation are formed autoregressively, can be formalized as

$$\pi_t^* = \tau(L) \pi_{t-1} + a_2. \tag{6.3}$$

This hypothesis will be referred to as "autoregressive expectations." If data on expectations were available one would proceed to estimate (6.2) and reject the hypothesis of autoregressive expectations if, and only if, one found $\psi(L)$ to be significantly different from zero.

Unfortunately, the expected rate of inflation is not directly observable. It does, however, enter market demand and supply schedules, and thus is reflected in market prices. In particular, I assume the validity of the Fisher relation,

$$r_t + \rho_t + \pi_t^* \tag{6.4}$$

where ρ_t is the real rate of interest in period t. I further assume that we can regard the real rate of interest as constant. The hypothesis (6.3) of autoregressive expectations can now be tested against the alternative hypothesis (6.2) of consistent expectations by substituting (6.2) into (6.4) and testing for the significance of $\psi(L)$ in the regression equation.

$$r_t = (a_1 + \rho) + \delta(L) \pi_{t-1} + \psi(L) m_{t-1}. \tag{6.5}$$

Estimates of (6.5) using four alternative market rates of interest as dependent variables are reported in Section 3.4. In every case I am forced to reject the hypothesis of autoregressive expectations in favor of the hypothesis of consistent expectations.

For several reasons it is of interest to examine an alternative model in which the interest rate on the left-hand side of (6.5) is an "expected," or implicit forward rate of interest. This will lend itself readily to examination of the term structure in Chapter 5, and will serve to make the assumption of constant real rate of interest less heroic in light of the transitory effect of changes in the money supply on the real rate. I assume that the expectations theory holds exactly, i.e., that an n-period spot force of interest is equal to the geometric mean of n one-period forces of interest. From this relation we can derive a measure of the implicit forward rate of interest for period $t + 1$,

$$r_{t+1} = \frac{(1 + R_{t+1})^2}{(1 + R_t)} - 1.0. \tag{6.6}$$

If we operate on (6.5) with L^{-1} —shift it forward one period—and apply Wold's chain principle of forecasting[a] we obtain the equation,

$$r_{t+1} = (a_1 + \rho) + \delta_1(L)\pi_{t-1} + \psi_1(L)m_{t-1}. \tag{6.7}$$

Estimates[b] of (6.7) are presented in Table 3-1. The F-statistic for the null-hypothesis ($\psi_1(L) = 0$) is of value $F = 17.16$; we are forced to reject the hypothesis of autoregressive expectations in favor of the alternative hypothesis of consistent expectations.

These results, taken together, imply that the claim that autoregressive models of forecast formation are misspecified is not a hollow one; this throws the results of tests carried out under autoregressive assumptions into serious question.

A related issue is examined; I find no evidence of long lags in the formation of expectations.

Chapter 4 is designed to analyze and test a much stronger hypothesis about forecasts of inflation, "rational expectations." The test of consistent expectations presented in Chapter 3 is a test of whether or not a potential source of information is reflected in the market rate of interest. In Chapter 4 we are concerned with the form of the function by which investors translate information about past money growth rates and past rates of inflation into forecasts of inflation. The chapter begins with a brief summary of Muth's paper[6] in which he introduced the notion that the predictions of investors are similar to the forecasts of the academic economist. This view recognized that investors gather

---

[a]That is, replace all variables on the r.h.s. by their expected values. The principle was developed by Wold.[5]

[b]r_{t+1} is calculated as shown in (6.6) with R_{t+1} equal to the six-month Treasury Bill rate and R_t equal to the three month Treasury Bill rate.

costly information and produce forecasts in order to maximize profits, in the way introduced in Chapter 3. Expectations, then, should depend on the structure of the process generating the variable to be predicted. The hypothesis of rational expectations, which states "that expectations of firms . . . tend to be distributed, for the same information set, about the prediction of the theory,"[7] naturally leads to the specification of models in which forecasts are formed in a manner analogous to the predictions of the economist, via reduced form relationships reflecting the structure of the economy. Indeed, this is the way in which Muth outlined his hypothesis. By coincidence, however, the rational expectation formula derived from his illustrative model was reducible to an autoregression. In this chapter I argue that this is the second major reason for the recent proliferation of autoregressive models of expectation formation; economists have remembered Muth's result, but not his analysis.

Section 4.1 presents a summary of Nelson's analysis of rational expectations. Nelson shows that in the general case rational expectations are not expressible as autoregressions, and that rational expectations are, in general, more efficient than autoregressive expectations.

Section 4.2 presents a simple eight equation textbook model of the macro-economy which incorporates the assumption that income is always at the full employment level. This leads to the reduced form expression for the rate of inflation

$$\pi_t = a_0 + \theta \phi(L) m_t + \gamma \xi(L) v_t, \tag{6.1}$$

which is recognized to be equivalent to (6.1) derived in Chapter 3. The rational expectation can be expressed, for π_t, as

$$\pi_t^* = a_1 + \delta(L) \pi_{t-1} + \psi(L) m_{t-1}. \tag{6.2}$$

If we substitute π_t, the actual rate of inflation, into the left-hand side of (6.2), the latter—interpreted as a regression equation—will tell us how a rational expectation would be formed given the information set containing past realized rates of inflation and money growth. Suppose that investors' expectations are actually formed, for the same information set, according to

$$\pi_t^* = a_1' + \delta'(L) \pi_{t-1} + \psi'(L) m_{t-1}, \tag{6.8}$$

where the primes indicate that the lag polynomials may be different than those in (6.2). Since the nominal rate of interest is determined by actual investors' expectations, under the assumption of constant real rate the market rate of interest equals a constant plus the r.h.s. of (6.8);

$$r_t = (a_1' + \rho) + \delta'(L) \pi_{t-1} + \psi'(L) m_{t-1}. \tag{6.9}$$

The test of the hypothesis of rational expectations in this model was shown to be a test of the equality of the lag polynomials in (6.8), with their counterparts in the version of (6.2), with actual inflation on the left-hand side. This is equivalent to a test that the coefficients of the lag polynomials in money growth and past inflation in

$$r_t - \pi_t = (a_1' + \rho - a_1) + (\delta'(L) - \delta(L))\pi_{t-1} \tag{6.10}$$

$$+ (\psi'(L) - \psi(L))m_{t-1}$$

are equal to zero, against the alternative hypothesis that they are not equal to zero. The results presented in Chapter 4 using the three month Treasury Bill rate indicate that we are unable to reject the hypothesis of rational expectations at any reasonable significance level.

I also show in Section 4.3 that an analogous test using the forward rate of interest r_{t+1} would be to test whether or not the lag distributions are equal to zero in

$$r_{t+1} - \pi_{t+1} = (a_1' + \rho - a_1) + (\delta_1'(L) - \delta_1(L))\pi_{t-1} \tag{6.11}$$

$$+ (\psi'(L) - \psi_1(L))m_{t-1}.$$

An estimate of (6.11) using quarterly U.S. data over the sample period 1953:I–1972:II is presented in Table 4-3. r_{t+1} was computed as in (6.6). The value of the F-statistic for the regression, $F = 1.01$, indicates that we are unable to reject the hypothesis of rational expectations in this model.

Section 4.4 of Chapter 4 adopts a "crude" quantity theory model of the determination of the rate of inflation. Tests of the rationality of expectations of inflation in this model yield similar results; I am unable to reject the hypothesis of rational expectations in any case.

A related issue is explored in Section 4.5. The assumption of constant real rate of interest is replaced with an autoregressive model of the determination of the real rate. Tests of rational expectations are performed using both forward and spot rates of interest. The results are uniformly consistent with the hypothesis of rational expectations. The relation between my work and a recent paper by Modigliani and Schiller[8] is explored in this section.

Chapter 5 presents an analysis concerning announcement effects and the term structure of interest rates under the assumption of rational expectations of inflation. I relax the assumptions concerning the exogenous disturbances in the earlier models to allow for nonzero expected values in future periods. The term structure of one-period rates of inflation is defined and compared with the marginal yield curve of the literature on the term structure of interest rates.

Section 5.2 presents a discussion of the attempt of the Federal Reserve

System to twist the yield curve in the early 'sixties. I discuss the relationship between the segmented markets hypothesis and the expectations theory of the term structure, and point out that twisting the yield curve is usually associated with the former hypothesis.

In Section 5.3 a model is developed based on (1) the expectations theory of the term structure and (2) rational expectations of inflation. I argue that in this model the shape and position of the yield curve are largely determined by the anticipated behavior of the exogenous disturbances in the model, hence on the announcements of the Federal Reserve System concerning future monetary policy.

Section 5.4 explores the possibility of achieving a target yield curve by choosing the appropriate announcements about future monetary policy. The result indicates that there exist many combinations of announcements concerning the future paths of exogenous variables that can achieve a given yield curve, but that the yield curve cannot be maintained over time.

In summary, this study has concerned the way in which investors process information in order to forecast inflation. I have argued that the misspecification of expectations models using autoregressive formulations is, if expectations are actually formed in a more sophisticated manner, a serious one. The evidence presented in this study indicates that expectations of investors reflect information on past money growth rates, and that these expectations of inflation are rational, in the sense of Muth, in a wide variety of models. There remains, nevertheless, a need for much additional work. In particular, more adequate specification of the real rate of interest will enable one to perform more reliable tests about the formation of expectations of inflation. The real rate of return appears as an endogenous variable in a full specification of the structure of the economy, and can be expressed by a corresponding reduced-form relationship. From this, one could obtain the rational expectation of the real rate of return, and substitute this variable for the real rate in Equation (6.9). Since I argue that investors gather information on the structure generating inflation, consistency requires a model in which investors can also acquire information about the process generating the real rate of return.

In addition, since the evidence presented in this study suggests that all previous work using autoregressive specifications of expected inflation is guilty of specification error, the results of tests performed using these specifications are suspect. This implies that the tests should be performed again employing specifications of expected inflation similar to the models of consistent expectations and rational expectations developed in this study. It is of interest to see whether or not the results of such tests are sensitive to the particular form of the forecasting mechanism employed.

Appendixes

Appendix

Period	3mTB	6mTB	r_{t+1}	PCP	AAA	m_t	π_t
53:I	2.018	1.900		2.310	3.070		
53:II	2.200	2.440	2.681	2.670	3.340	2.508	2.116
53:III	2.088	2.120	2.152	2.750	3.240	0.624	3.509
53:IV	1.427	1.340	1.253	2.310	3.110	0.312	1.391
54:I	0.984	0.750	0.517	2.000	2.950	1.244	−1.386
54:II	0.782	0.590	0.398	1.580	2.880	0.928	0.000
54:III	0.892	0.760	0.628	1.330	2.870	3.708	0.000
54:IV	0.948	0.910	0.872	1.310	2.890	4.288	−1.739
55:I	1.177	1.390	1.603	1.680	2.930	4.544	−0.699
55:II	1.491	1.530	1.569	2.000	3.040	2.396	−0.350
55:III	1.876	2.100	2.324	2.330	3.110	1.788	1.051
55:IV	2.225	2.640	3.057	2.810	3.100	0.592	1.747
56:I	2.372	2.410	2.448	3.000	3.080	1.480	−1.391
56:II	2.650	2.650	2.650	3.270	3.280	0.884	2.792
56:III	2.606	3.010	3.416	3.280	3.430	0.296	4.853
56:IV	3.000	3.540	4.083	3.630	3.690	1.764	3.082
57:I	3.165	3.420	3.676	3.630	3.670	0.880	1.699
57:II	3.040	3.630	4.221	3.630	3.740	0.000	3.723
57:III	3.404	4.090	4.781	3.980	4.100	0.292	5.700
57:IV	3.337	3.410	3.483	4.070	4.080	−2.336	0.331
58:I	1.562	1.270	0.979	2.630	3.590	−0.292	4.624
58:II	1.046	0.640	0.236	1.710	3.570	4.408	3.592
58:III	1.686	2.780	3.886	1.960	3.850	4.068	0.324
58:IV	2.756	2.830	2.904	3.080	4.090	4.892	0.000
59:I	2.712	3.100	3.489	3.260	4.140	4.264	0.000
59:II	2.851	3.450	4.052	3.560	4.370	3.656	0.970
59:III	3.358	4.430	5.513	3.970	4.430	1.952	2.581
59:IV	4.209	4.585	4.962	4.670	4.560	−3.052	2.564
60:I	3.945	4.321	4.689	4.660	4.560	−1.676	0.000
60:II	3.392	3.684	3.977	4.250	4.460	−3.928	2.229
60:III	2.286	2.574	2.863	3.340	4.280	1.132	0.950
60:IV	2.384	2.650	2.917	3.280	4.310	0.564	2.528
61:I	2.408	2.601	2.794	3.030	4.270	1.976	0.314
61:II	2.228	2.436	2.584	2.760	4.270	3.088	−0.314
61:III	2.402	2.670	2.939	2.920	4.450	2.228	1.884
61:IV	2.458	2.686	2.915	2.980	4.390	3.880	1.250
62:I	2.752	2.955	3.158	3.220	4.420	2.196	0.623
62:II	2.694	2.789	2.884	3.160	4.280	1.640	1.555
62:III	2.837	3.005	3.173	3.300	4.350	−0.816	1.239

Period	3mTB	6mTB	r_{t+1}	PCP	AAA	m_t	π_t
62:IV	2.803	2.875	2.947	3.230	4.250	2.180	1.853
63:I	2.916	2.970	3.024	3.250	4.190	4.336	0.307
63:II	2.920	3.006	3.092	3.250	4.220	3.752	0.307
63:III	3.320	3.437	3.554	3.720	4.290	3.452	3.337
63:IV	3.522	3.648	3.774	3.880	4.330	4.212	1.218
64:I	3.532	3.664	3.796	3.880	4.360	2.604	0.607
64:II	3.482	3.612	3.742	3.890	4.410	3.364	0.909
64:III	3.506	3.618	3.730	3.880	4.410	6.420	2.116
65:IV	3.624	3.794	3.964	4.020	4.430	4.800	1.203
65:I	3.929	4.003	4.077	4.270	4.410	2.748	0.600
65:II	3.895	3.950	4.005	4.380	4.440	2.976	2.695
65:III	3.836	3.938	4.040	4.380	4.490	4.676	1.487
65:IV	4.082	4.238	4.394	4.380	4.600	6.568	1.481
66:I	4.670	4.820	4.970	4.880	4.780	6.224	0.590
66:II	4.642	4.814	4.986	5.390	4.980	4.716	7.369
66:III	4.932	5.189	5.447	5.850	5.310	−0.932	4.342
66:IV	5.344	5.604	5.865	6.000	4.350	0.232	2.577
67:I	4.555	4.565	4.576	5.380	5.030	3.500	0.853
67:II	3.604	3.808	4.012	4.670	5.240	6.708	2.839
67:III	4.275	4.821	5.370	5.000	5.620	9.328	4.510
67:IV	4.762	5.286	5.813	5.280	6.070	5.560	3.066
68:I	4.969	5.144	5.319	5.500	6.100	5.044	3.873
68:II	5.621	5.785	5.949	6.180	6.270	8.228	4.384
68:III	5.095	5.224	5.353	5.880	6.020	8.700	5.420
68:IV	5.492	5.618	5.741	5.920	6.190	6.852	4.813
69:I	6.156	6.309	6.462	6.620	6.660	6.740	4.227
69:II	6.077	6.149	6.221	7.350	6.790	5.020	6.797
69:III	7.007	7.194	7.381	8.330	6.970	2.180	6.170
69:IV	7.193	7.565	7.938	8.460	7.350	1.184	5.316
70:I	7.164	7.249	7.334	8.550	7.930	3.932	6.246
70:II	7.035	7.262	7.489	8.230	8.110	7.012	6.396
70:III	6.412	6.526	6.640	7.900	8.130	5.168	4.116
70:IV	5.288	5.422	5.556	6.300	8.050	3.780	5.273
71:I	3.773	3.806	3.839	4.470	7.080	7.300	3.075
71:II	4.139	4.367	4.596	5.100	7.530	11.300	4.695
71:III	5.078	5.363	5.649	5.730	7.590	7.700	4.408
71:IV	4.191	4.338	4.485	4.920	7.260	0.400	1.606
72:I	3.180	3.594	4.010	3.930	7.270	5.900	3.886
72:II	3.648	4.064	4.482	4.510	7.300	8.000	2.264

Sources

Three month Treasury Bills ($3mTB$) and six month Treasury Bills ($6mTB$) are averages computed from daily closing bid prices. Bills are quoted on bank discount basis. When the six month Treasury Bill rate was not available—they were not regularly issued before December, 1958—the market yield on taxable Treasury Notes, with six remaining months to maturity, was used. Data were obtained from the *Federal Reserve Bulletin.*

The expected three month interest rate for period (t + 1), r_{t+1}, was calculated from three month and six month Treasury Bill rates according to Equation (3.22) of Chapter 3, with $n = 1$.

Four to six month Prime Commercial Paper rates, *PCP*, are averages of daily offering rates of dealers and were obtained from the *Federal Reserve Bulletin.*

Rates on Corporate *AAA* bonds, *AAA*, are averages of daily figures, and were obtained from the *Federal Reserve Bulletin.*

The percent rate of change in $M1$, m_t, was calculated from the 1968 revision of seasonally adjusted $M1$ (currency plus demand deposits); data were obtained as follows. (1) 1953-1963 figures were obtained from the December, 1970 *Federal Reserve Bulletin*, pp. 895-909. (2) 1964-1970 figures were obtained from the November, 1971 *Federal Reserve Bulletin*, pp. 884-885. (3) 1971-1972 figures were obtained from the December, 1972 *Federal Reserve Bulletin.*

The percent rate of change in consumer prices, π_t, was computed from the Consumer Price Index—Bureau of Labor Statistics index for city wage-earners and clerical workers—as obtained from the *Federal Reserve Bulletin.*

Notes

Notes

Chapter 1
Introduction

1. Maurice Allais, *Économie et Intèrêt* (Paris: Librairie des Publications Officielles, 1947), p. 37.

2. John R. Hicks, *Value and Capital* (Oxford: Oxford University Press, 1939), pp. 159-160.

3. Harry Johnson, *Macroeconomics and Monetary Theory* (Chicago: Aldine Publishing Company, 1972), p. 56.

4. S.J. Turnovsky and M.L. Wachter, "A Test of the Expectations Hypothesis Using Directly Observed Wage and Price Expectations" *Staff Economic Studies*, Volume 63 (Washington, D.C.: Board of Governors of the Federal Reserve, February 1971), p. 1.

5. William Gibson, "Price Expectations Effects on Interest Rates" *Journal of Finance*, 25 (March 1970), p. 19.

6. John F. Muth, "Rational Expectations and the Theory of Price Movements" *Econometrica*, 29, no. 3 (July 1961), pp. 315-335.

7. Robert Mundell, *Monetary Theory* (New York: Goodyear, 1972), p. 78.

Chapter 2
Review of Previous Work on Expectations

1. E.J. Burtt, *Social Perspectives in the History of Economic Theory* (New York: St. Martin's Press, 1972), p. 22 (emphasis added).

2. John Locke, *An Essay Concerning Human Understanding* (Cleveland, Ohio: Meridian Books, 1964), p. 402.

3. Ibid., p. 405 (emphasis added).

4. Ibid., p. 405 (emphasis added).

5. Alfred Marshall, *Money, Credit, and Commerce* (London: Macmillan and Company, 1923), p. 76 (emphasis added).

6. Ibid., p. 256 (emphasis added).

7. John M. Keynes, *A Treatise on Money* (London: Macmillan and Company, 1930), p. 159 (emphasis added).

8. Ibid., p. 160 (emphasis added).

9. Ibid., p. 202 (emphasis added).

10. Ibid., p. 212.

11. Ibid., p. 264.

12. John F. Muth, "Rational Expectations and the Theory of Price Movements," *Econometrica*, 29, no. 3 (July 1961), pp. 315-335. I gratefully acknowledge permission to quote from this innovative paper.

13. Ibid., p. 316.

14. Ibid., p. 317.

15. Ibid., p. 316.

16. Charles R. Nelson, "The Structure of Rational Expectations: Implications for the Predictive Efficiency of Economic Models and the Empirical Specification of Expectations Mechanisms," (Chicago: Center for Mathematical Studies in Business and Economics Report 7209, 1972), p. 1.

17. Allen A. Walters, "Consistent Expectations, Distributed Lags, and the Quantity Theory," *The Economic Journal*, 81, no. 322 (June 1971), pp. 273-281. I would like to thank the Editors of *The Economic Journal* for permission to quote from this paper.

18. Ibid., p. 273, fn. 1.

19. Ibid., p. 273.

20. Ibid., pp. 273-274 (emphasis added).

21. Ibid., p. 274.

22. Ibid., p. 275.

23. Ibid., p. 276 (emphasis added).

24. Ibid., p. 281.

25. Charles R. Nelson, *The Term Structure of Interest Rates* (New York: Basic Books, 1972).

26. Nelson, "Rational Expectations."

27. Ibid., p. 1.

28. Ibid., p. 4 (emphasis added).

29. Ibid., p. 12 (emphasis added).

30. Ibid., pp. 20-21.

31. See, for example, Fama's review article, "Efficient Capital Markets: A Review of Theoretical and Empirical Work," *Journal of Finance: Papers and Proceedings* (May 1970), pp. 383-417.

32. Irving Fisher, *The Theory of Interest* (New York: Macmillan and Company, 1930). I wish to acknowledge the kind permission of Irving N. Fisher to quote from this pathbreaking study.

33. John Stuart Mill, *Principles of Political Economy*, ed. Ashley (London: Longmans, Green, 1923), p. 436.

34. Fisher, *Interest*, p. 494 (emphasis added).

35. Ibid., p. 494 (emphasis added).

36. Ibid., p. 400.

37. Ibid., pp. 405-406 (emphasis added).

38. Ibid., p. 416 (emphasis added).

39. Ibid., p. 44 (emphasis added).

40. Ibid., p. 416 (emphasis added).

41. Ibid., p. 419.

42. Ibid., p. 423.

43. Ibid., p. 423 (emphasis added).

44. Arthur Laffer and J. Richard Zecher, "Anticipations About the Value of Money–Much Ado About Nothing?" (Mimeographed, University of Chicago, 1971).

45. Ibid., p. 17.

46. Ibid., p. 17.

47. Irving Fisher, *Interest*, p. 429 (emphasis added).

48. Milton Friedman, *The Optimum Quantity of Money and Other Essays* (Chicago: Aldine Publishing Company, 1969), p. 100.

49. Phillip Cagan, "The Monetary Dynamics of Hyperinflation" in *Studies in the Quantity Theory of Money*, ed. Milton Friedman (Chicago: University of Chicago Press, 1956).

50. Milton Friedman, *A Theory of the Consumption Function* (Princeton, N.J.: Princeton University Press [for NBER], 1957).

51. Phillip Cagan, "Hyperinflations," p. 77 (emphasis added).

52. R.J. Ball, "Some Econometric Analysis of the Long-Term Rate of Interest in the United Kingdom, 1921-61," *The Manchester School of Economics and Social Studies*, 33 (January 1965), pp. 45-96.

53. Richard Roll, "Interest Rates on Monetary Assets and Price Index Changes," *Journal of Finance: Papers and Proceedings*, 27, no. 2 (May 1972), pp. 251-278. I wish to thank the Editors of *The Journal of Finance* for permission to quote this study.

54. William Gibson, "Price Expectations Effects on Interest Rates," *Journal of Finance*, 25 (March 1970), pp. 19-32.

55. Thomas J. Sargent, "Commodity Price Expectations and the Interest Rate," *Quarterly Journal of Economics*, 83 (February 1969), pp. 127-140.

56. Von Jürgens Siebke und Manfred Wellms, "Zinsniveau, Geldpolitik und Inflation," *Kredit und Kapital*, Heft 2 (1972), pp. 171-205.

57. Leonall C. Andersen and Keith M. Carlson, "A Monetarist Model for Economic Stabilization," Federal Reserve Bank of St. Louis *Review* (April 1970), pp. 7-21.

58. Martin S. Feldstein and Otto Eckstein, "The Fundamental Determinants of the Interest Rate," *Review of Economics and Statistics*, 52 (November 1970), pp. 363-376.

59. William P. Yohe and Denis L. Karnosky, "Interest Rates and Price Level Changes, 1952-1969," Federal Reserve Bank of St. Louis *Review* 51 (December 1969), pp. 18-36.

60. Robert J. Gordon, "Econometric Techniques and Economic Common Sense," (Mimeographed, University of Chicago, 1972).

61. S.J. Turnovsky, "Some Empirical Evidence on the Formation of Price Expectations," *Journal of the American Statistical Association*, 65 (December 1970), pp. 1441-1454.

62. Franco Modigliani and Robert J. Schiller, "Inflation, Rational Expectations, and the Term Structure of Interest Rates," *Economica*, 40, no. 157 (February 1973), pp. 12-43.

63. John F. Muth, "Optimal Properties of Exponentially Weighted Forecasts," *Journal of the American Statistical Association*, 55 (June 1960), pp. 299-306.

64. Marc Nerlove, "Distributed Lags and Demand Analysis," *Agriculture Handbook Number 141*, (Washington, D.C.: Dept. of Agriculture, 1958).

65. Milton Friedman, *Consumption Function*.

66. Arnold Zellner, D.S. Huang and L.C. Chau, "Further Analysis of the Short-Run Consumption Function with Emphasis on the Role of Liquid Assets," *Econometrica*, 83, no. 3 (July 1965), pp. 571-581.

67. Franco Modigliani and Richard C. Sutch, "Debt Management and the Term Structure of Interest Rates: An Empirical Analysis of Recent Experience," *Journal of Political Economy*, 75 (1967), pp. 569-589.

68. Z. Griliches and Neil Wallace, "The Determinants of Investment Revisited," *International Economic Review*, 6 (1965), pp. 311-329.

69. Modigliani and Schiller, "Rational Expectations."

70. Charles R. Nelson, *Term Structure*.

71. R.H. Raasche and H.T. Shapiro, "The FRB-MIT Model: Its Special Features," *American Economic Review, Papers and Proceedings* (May 1968), pp. 123-149.

72. Anderson and Carlson, "Monetarist Model."

73. David Laidler, "The Phillips Curve, Expectations, and Incomes Policy," in *The Current Inflation*, ed. H.G. Johnson and N. Nobay (London: St. Martin's Press, 1971), p. 88.

74. Richard Roll, "Interest Rates on Monetary Assets and Price Index Changes," *Journal of Finance, Papers and Proceedings*, 27, no. 2 (May 1972), p. 266.

75. Thomas J. Sargent, "Commodity Price Expectations and· the Interest Rate," *Quarterly Journal of Economics*, 83 (February 1969), pp. 127-140.

76. Ball, "Econometric Analysis."

77. Yohe and Karnosky, "Interest Rates."

78. Feldstein and Eckstein, "Fundamental Determinants."

79. Donald L. Tuttle and William L. Wilbur, "A Multivariate Time Series Investigation of Annual Returns on Highest Grade Corporate Bonds," *Journal of Financial and Quantitative Analysis*, 6 (March 1971), pp. 707-721.

80. Duncan K. Foley and Miguel Sidrauski, *Monetary and Fiscal Policy in a Growing Economy* (Toronto: Macmillan and Company, 1971), p. 33 (emphasis added).

81. Nelson, "Rational Expectations," p. 25.

82. Patrick Hendershott and G. Horwich, "The Appropriate Indicators of Monetary Policy: Part II," in *Savings and Residential Financing: 1969 Conference Proceedings*, ed. D.P. Jacobs (New York: United States Savings and Loan League, 1969), p. 44.

83. Milton Friedman and Anna Schwartz, "Trends in Money, Income, and Prices; 1867-1966," (unpublished study for NBER, 1967), Chapter 4, p. 141.

84. Thomas J. Sargent, "Interest Rates and Prices in the Long-Run: A Study of the Gibson Paradox" (Mimeographed, Board of Governors of the Federal Reserve, 1971), p. 25. Sargent refers to the estimated thirty year lag of commercial paper rates on inflation found by Fisher for U.S. data. In fairness to Fisher, however, the *total* lag was found to be thirty years; the *mean* lag was estimated to be about ten years, still a candidate for the "molasses world."

85. Yohe and Karnosky, "Interest Rates."

86. A.R. Soltow and Dudley G. Luckett, "Determinants of Interest Rate Expectations," *Journal of Money, Credit and Banking*, 4 (May 1972), p. 274.

87. Karl Brunner and Allen Meltzer, "Friedman's Monetary Theory," *Journal of Political Economy*, 80, no. 5 (September-October 1972), p. 837.

88. Foley and Sidrauski, p. 33.

89. S.J. Turnovsky, "Some Empirical Evidence on the Formation of Price Expectations," op. cit., p. 1444. I wish to thank the Editors of the *Journal of the American Statistical Association* for permission to quote this paper.

90. Andersen and Carlson, "Monetarist Model," p. 24.

Chapter 3
Optimal Use of Information

1. Robert A. Mundell, *Monetary Theory* (New York: Goodyear, 1972), p. 78.

2. Charles R. Nelson, "The Structure of Rational Expectations: Implications for the Predictive Efficiency of Economic Models and the Empirical Specification of Expectations Mechanisms (Mimeographed, University of Chicago, 1972), p. 13.

3. Ibid., p. 13.

4. For example see Phillip Cagan, "The Monetary Dynamics of Hyperinflation," in *Studies in the Quantity Theory of Money*, ed. Milton Friedman (Chicago: University of Chicago Press, 1956); Martin S. Feldstein and Otto Eckstein, "The Fundamental Determinants of the Interest Rate," *Review of Economics and Statistics*, 52 (November 1970), pp. 363-376; William Gibson, "Price Expectations Effects on Interest Rates," *Journal of Finance*, 25 (March 1970), pp. 19-34; Franco Madigliani and Robert J. Schiller, "Inflation, Rational Expectations, and the Term Structure of Interest Rates," *Economica*, 40, no. 157 (February 1973), pp. 12-43.

5. Milton Friedman, *A Theoretical Framework for Monetary Analysis* (New York: National Bureau of Economic Research, 1971), p. 40.

6. See, for example, Friedrich Lutz, *The Theory of Interest*, trans. C. Wittich (Chicago: Aldine Publishing Company, 1968).

7. Herman Wold, "Forecasting by the Chain Principle," in *Proceedings of the Symposium on Time Series Analysis*, ed. Rosenblatt (New York: 1963).

8. Robert Mundell, "Inflation and Real Interest," *Journal of Political Economy*, 71 (June 1963), pp. 280-283.

9. Thomas J. Sargent, "Commodity Price Expectations and the Interest Rate," *Quarterly Journal of Economics*, 83 (February 1969), p. 127.

10. Milton Friedman, *The Optimum Quantity of Money and Other Essays* (Chicago: Aldine Publishing Company, 1969), p. 100.

Chapter 4
Rational Expectations of Inflation

1. John F. Muth, "Rational Expectations and the Theory of Price Movements," *Econometrica*, 29, no. 3 (July 1961), p. 316.

2. Ibid., pp. 315-335.

3. Charles R. Nelson, "The Structure of Rational Expectations: Implications for the Predictive Efficiency of Economic Models and the Empirical Specification of Expectations Mechanisms (Mimeographed, University of Chicago, 1972), p. 2.

4. Ibid.

5. This property is proved in Charles R. Nelson, "Rational Expectations," pp. 8-14.

6. Ibid., p. 2.

7. Ibid., p. 12.

8. Milton Friedman, *A Theoretical Framework for Monetary Analysis* (New York: National Bureau of Economic Research, 1971), pp. 29-31.

9. Bennett T. McCallum, "Friedman's Missing Equation: Another Approach," *The Manchester School* (forthcoming).

10. Milton Friedman, *Theoretical Framework*, p. 81.

11. Paul Samuelson, *Foundations of Economic Analysis* (New York: Atheneum, 1971), pp. 330-331 (emphasis added).

12. Robert E. Lucas, Jr., "Econometric Testing of the Natural Rate Hypothesis," in *The Econometrics of Price Determination* (Washington, D.C.: Board of Governors of the Federal Reserve System, 1972).

13. Franco Modigliani, and Richard C. Sutch, "Innovations in Interest Rate Policy," *American Economic Review: Papers and Proceedings*, 56 (1966), pp. 178-197; Franco Modigliani and Richard C. Sutch, "Debt Management and the Term Structure of Interest Rate: An Empirical Analysis of Recent Experience," *Journal of Political Economy*, 75 (1967), pp. 569-589.

14. Franco Modigliani, and Robert J. Schiller, "Inflation, Rational Expectations, and the Term Structure of Interest Rates," *Economica*, 40, no. 157 (February 1973).

15. John Rutledge, "Modigliani and Schiller and Rational Expectations," (Mimeographed, University of Virginia, 1973).

16. Modigliani and Schiller, "Rational Expectations," p. 13.

Chapter 5
Announcement Effects and Rational Expectations

1. Milton Friedman, "Time Perspective in the Demand for Money" (Mimeographed, University of Chicago, 1972).

2. See, for example, Jacob B. Michaelsen, *The Term Structure of Interest Rates* (New York: Intext Educational Publishers, 1973); Franco Modigliani and Richard C. Sutch, "Debt-Management and the Term Structure of Interest Rates: An Empirical Analysis of Recent Experience," *Journal of Political Economy*, 75 (1967), pp. 569-589.

3. David Meiselman, *The Term Structure of Interest Rates* (Englewood Cliffs, N.J.: Prentice-Hall, Inc., 1962).

4. Paul Samuelson, in, American Bankers Association, *Proceedings of a Symposium on Money, Interest Rates, and Economic Activity* (New York: American Bankers Association, 1967), p. 33.

5. David Meiselman, in *Savings and Residential Finance: 1968 Conference Proceedings*, ed. D.P. Jacobs and R.T. Pratt (Chicago: United States Savings and Loan League, 1968).

Chapter 6
Conclusions

1. John F. Muth, "Rational Expectations and the Theory of Price Movements," *Econometrica*, 29, no. 3 (July 1961), pp. 315-335.

2. A.A. Walters, "Consistent Expectations, Distributed Lags, and the Quantity Theory," *The Economic Journal*, 81, no. 322 (June 1971), pp. 273-281.

3. Charles R. Nelson, "The Structure of Rational Expectations: Implications for the Predictive Efficiency of Economic Models and the Empirical Specification of Expectations Mechanisms," (Mimeographed, University of Chicago, 1972).

4. Irving Fisher, *The Theory of Interest* (New York: The Macmillan Company, 1930).

5. Herman Wold, "Forecasting by the Chain Principle," in *Proceedings of the Symposium on Time Series Analysis*, ed. Rosenblatt (New York: 1963).

6. John F. Muth, "Rational Expectations."

7. Ibid., p. 316.

8. Franco Modigliani and Robert J. Schiller, "Inflation, Rational Expectations, and the Term Structure of Interest Rates," *Economica*, 40, no. 157 (February 1973), pp. 12-43.

Index

Index

Almon polynomial lag, 23, 69; estimates of, 41-42, 56-60, 63-65, 68
Announcement effects, 26, 73, 76;
choice of, 87-90
Autoregressive forecasts: of inflation,
29, 36, 39, 67; of real rate of return,
65-66; and rational expectations,
15-16, 24, 48-51

Cagan, Phillip, 21, 22
Chain principle of forecasting, 39,
56-62, 66-67, 96
Cochrane-Orcutt iterative technique,
43
Consistent expectations, 30, 34, 36,
39, 95; tests of, 40-43, 66-69, 94-96

Distributed lag, 20, 23, 54-55, 62, 74;
Almon polynomial, 23, 69; estimates
of Almon polynomial, 41-42, 56-60,
68; geometric, 22, 43

Economies of scale in forecasting, 33
Error-learning models of forecasting,
16, 23
Expectations theory, 37-38, 59, 64,
81-83, 99

Fisher, Irving, 17, 18, 94
Fisher relation, 30, 34, 57, 95; for
forward interest rates, 38, 58, 85;
for term structure, 89
Forecast production, 7, 23, 27-30, 93
Forward interest rates, 30, 37-39, 58,
67, 82-88
Forward shift operator, 56, 66-67, 75;
definition of, 38-39
Friedman, Milton, 21-22, 25, 36, 78

Geometric lag, 22, 43; see also Distributed lag

Inflation, 29; determinants of, 34,
49-50, 52-55; optimal forecasts of,
30-32; quantity theory of money
and, 61-65, 98; reduced-form equations for, 34, 49, 52-55, 74-75;
structural model of, 52-55

Keynes, John M., 9, 10

Lag operator, 22, 35
Lag polynomials, 34-35, 48-51, 55-56,
98; invertibility conditions for, 35,
50-51, 55
Liquidity effect, 37, 96
Locke, John, 8

Marshall, Alfred, 9
Mean of lag distributions, 17, 20-21,
24-25, 30, 43-44
Muth, John F., 4, 11-12, 48-49, 96

Nelson, Charles R., 12, 14, 24, 49, 52n

Operation Twist, 78-83, 99
Optimal forecast production, 30-32

Preferred habitat theory, 80-81

Quantity theory of money, 61-65, 98

Rational expectations: and autoregressive models, 15-16, 24, 48-51; definition of, 48; Muth and, 4, 11-12,
48-49, 96; tests of, 55-61, 61-65,
65-70, 68, 96-98
Real rates of interest, 19, 21, 36, 58,
95, 97; autoregressive specification
for, 65-70, 98; and liquidity effect,
37, 96; and nominal interest rates, 1,
19
Reduced-form equations, 34, 49,
52-55, 74-75

Segmented markets hypothesis, 80
Specification errors in forecasting
models, 24-27, 30, 45, 52n, 71
Stochastic process, 34, 48-51, 74

Term to maturity structure: of expected inflation, 77-78, 86-87, 98;
of interest rates, 78, 98; of real interest rates, 88
Twisting the yield curve, 79-80; and
the expectations theory, 81-83;
feasibility of, 83, 87, 91; and Operation Twist, 6, 78-83, 99; and the
segmented markets hypothesis, 80

Walters, A.A., 12, 13

About the Author

John Rutledge is assistant professor of economics at Tulane University. He received the B.A. with honors in economics from Lake Forest College in 1970 and the Ph.D. from the University of Virginia in 1973. He was elected to Phi Beta Kappa and has been a Woodrow Wilson Fellow and a Harold Stonier Fellow in Money and Banking. From 1970 to 1973, Dr. Rutledge was editor of *Virginia Essays in Economics.*